GW00659208

STEVE AYLETT

SMITHEREENS

Steve Aylett is the author of
Slaughtermatic, LINT, Fain the Sorcerer,
Atom, The Crime Studio, Bigot Hall,
Rebel at the End of Time, Toxicology, The
Inflatable Volunteer, Shamanspace, And
Your Point Is?, The Complete Accomplice
and *Novahead.* He is also responsible for
the comics *The Caterer* and
Get That Thing Away From Me.

STEVE AYLETT
SMITHEREENS

SCAR GARDEN

SMITHEREENS

stories by Steve Aylett

copyright © Steve Aylett 2010

Pics by Steve Aylett

ISBN 978-0-9565677-1-0

www.steveaylett.com

scargardenmedia@yahoo.co.uk

CONTENTS

'Infinity has so much structure
it has no structure.'

Karloff's Circus

'Don't order the swordfish.'

The Ninth Configuration

ON READING NEW BOOKS

Enjoyment can be kept sharp by the outrage of others - sadly though, genuinely-felt outrage is as rare today as it's ever been. I rode out of a swirling vortex on a hell-pig the other day and people just stared.

It's a world where things created for comfort are used for denial and the dwindling comb-over of culture has led to books in which the protagonist is one or other kind of automated remnant. The inherent advantage of selling limitation is that one size is declared to fit all. Support is minimal for defiance in a world with charity toward none, malice for all and the bland decree that there can be no new ideas under the local sun.

When offered a handful of options by a manipulator, we should be careful (in turning directly away to look at the thousands of other options available) that we are not being cleverly positioned to miss the billions more in every other direction.

The truly new invents new guts for itself. An angel is unlikely to be boring or devout. The miraculous should be at least equal to the forbidden. That the two are often the same thing is one of the solitaire fucking diamonds of truth.

At its shallowest an epigram is merely a sentence which strikes a pose, the sort of prim wiseacreing that fades within decades, too flimsy to depend on. There are also stegobromides - very obvious but lightly encrypted truths which, due to people's preference for them in their obscured form, have been left to petrify inside their own code. Then there are sayings which connect up only by ignoring a lot of facts: views with square edges, cropping off bits of reality. These are even less useful than those messiest bit of folklore that are akin to tripping over a ball of snakes.

There are proverbs which are dumb and funny - human, in other words. And finally those sayings born from the compelling notion of a sentence, word or musical note which could cataclysmically open reality to even the most evasive mind. I like the last two varieties and scrawled a bunch for the sayings of Bingo Violaine, whom the citizens of Accomplice use as a sort of epigram Pez. It's fun to drop a profundity into a scene where screaming chimps are attacking a chef, or to bat a balloon dog into a philosophical discussion.

Imagine the horror of dropping into the world's throat while trusting others' declarations above the evidence of your own senses! Treason is disliked because it reveals the mechanism. In this case the mechanism is that of reality by decree - a mechanism toward which the cosmos is cryptically uncooperative. The truth doesn't actually require our attention - it persists with or without us. It's more indifferent to us than we can ever be to it. And when everyone dodges blame, that stuff remains in the air like radioactivity.

Imagine honest, clean regret.

In toxic times an honest eye is bound to result, for several years at least, in a sort of reverse-image horror at what's been perpetrated. The state stripped of crimes - not even a skeleton is left. This resentment is a stain left by clear perception. You become like the philosopher who repeatedly enraged Gurdjieff by shaking him awake at three in the morning. Amid drab masses seething with optimism, any true individual almost by definition won't be heard of - but they certainly exist and are a vivid, angular joy.

You can depart an empire by turning five corners, and ofcourse a one-track god is easily avoided. But as Eddie Gamete once said, the nightmare's likely to renew until the day humanity rests finally in lavender and ruins, becoming one big last outbreath. Patience.

BOSSANOVA

The plastic man missed his eyes more than a human might. He had used them often, had never deferred. But exploding consoles will have their due. Nobody had doubted the authenticity of his face until that little incident.

It took a while to get himself hooked directly into the cruiser's system and then he sensed something out there – a ship shaped like a hammer bent back upon itself. The crew judged the enemy battleship quite plain and stood by Bossanova as their Captain. He was surprised and touched. He had, after all, a nose like a slot car.

Professor Baum's weathered features transmitted as Bossanova stood on the stance platform. 'You will return to Earth with me.'

'Not a very interesting opinion,' the robot remarked.

'You're malfunctioning. That's why you're being so

obdurate. Well, you've made yourself an object of infamy. I can make no more excuses for you.'

'I wasn't aware you'd made any, father. What sort of stuff did you come up with?'

'Don't call me that. Not any more. You're a belief toy. Acquiescence covered in skin. There's no gadget monarchy. You're living in a fool's paradise of emoticons and sardonyx crystal.'

'Emoticons, unlike a face, say what they mean. Anyway, an act informed by the knowledge of ineffectiveness – is it stronger or weaker than a deluded one?'

'I'll not quarrel with a component,' said Baum, and paused.

'Weaker?' he ventured.

'It's exactly the same,' said Bossanova.

'Five minutes to fire-up. You won't prevent us using the Drive.'

'I won't need to,' said the plastic man in quiet disappointment. Baum had lost his easy manner and his passion.

What can make a person less wise as he grows older? thought Nova. Not the accumulation of knowledge but the loss of it. To relinquish so much and deny you ever possessed it – such weakness, cowardice. To come to believe his own lies. The mind is horribly willing to resign before its time.

Bossanova remembered how he'd sat in Baum's workshop as the Professor tooled around in smoked glasses, his motives already beginning to discolour at the edges. Nova was propped on a table, wearing a preliminary head like a military field-telephone. Baum tapped a stroheim dummy tricked out in a suit.

'Executive model. When he lies his nose doesn't get longer but his limo does, eh? But not enough to make it human. All those clockwork Asimovian equations, reasoning gears which must be clanked precisely into place before anything proceeds. A cagefight between liquid crystals.'

He lifted Nova's forehead like a visor. 'While in your case it's alot more fluid. Po-mo fluid. I thought of it when I read about court cases. It isn't an investigation. It's decided, not detected, that a person committed a crime – the fact of whether he actually did is not altered by the decision, but people will behave as if it is. The declaration revises reality – no other version has ever existed, and the notion of objective fact is at best a childish nonsense, at worst a punishable heresy.'

Nova panned around the lab as Baum bustled about. Baum came up with a hydraulic tweezer.

'Head still. Assembling eyelashes here.'

'Thank you, father. Please continue.'

'My po-mo suspension fluid operates on the principle that something is a fact by a human merely declaring that it is so. It's not even fancy. It's just erasure after erasure, a billion retroactive truths.' Baum carefully removed the skullnet.

'This way, when I tell you that you're lifting a crate, you immediately will be. The agony of disparity doesn't even arise – automatic accedence takes care of that. No reasoning need be done, and fewer parts are involved. All you are told, you will believe, negating all that was previously said and believed, and no contradiction.'

'Does this make me human, father?'

'Almost. We may also tell tales to ourselves, and believe. You will stand as my masterpiece.'

Bossanova left the workshop, a guarantee stamped on the flipside of his stomach.

But they had made the mistake of providing him with a set of senses, never guessing that he would use them to perceive the world as it was. Told that he would leave the room immediately, it took him only a few moments to perceive that he would not. He realised that if the mere statement that he would lift a crate meant that he would lift a crate, he need not be there when it was happening – if the statement truly created the fact, then somehow the crate would be lifted by him even if he was seven miles away staring at the ocean. He had been assured that it would be impossible for the crate not to be lifted by him. When his supervisors shouted at him that he had not lifted the crate, he reminded them that they had told him he would. By their own assertion, it was impossible that he hadn't. In regard to peers and authority, he effectively had a brain of cork, floating over their influence and absorbing nothing.

One day he walked through a wall, got in a truck and drove away despite his handlers' claims that he would not do so.

His winters of flowering were not easy, havocing through books and the world to find those rare places which retained some flavour.

He was drunk with each bit of reality he discovered, with every imperfection according to the law. Metallic goosebumps came up like pinheads.

He'd been born into a system which needed no reason, only motive; which was moved not by goals but by the need to perpetually evade. It was fact by decree, irrespective of actual fact. This wankers' charter had its merits when it came to social control in human society. Proclamation surpassed raw observation as a matter of course. It required millions to live a spineless incoherence.

Bossanova, his head a chipped chesspiece, passed years studying this chilling nonsense. He suggested that the multiple erasures of ungrounded belief was finally a stem broken in a thousand places – nothing would grow again. And so he'd ended up as an outlandish, injection-moulded pirate, dangerous by virtue of dealing in reality which surpassed the recommended dose. His crew were a bunch of people with minds of their own.

Other pomo droids were sense-neutered and did whatever was demanded of them. Baum's suspension fluid was seen as a magic pill. If the principle on which it was based was what made it work, then wonders could be worked by decree.

The Decree Drive was installed in a battle cruiser and the honoured Professor Baum went along for the first spin. The flight was not referred to as an experiment, as that would imply that what was believed might not occur. Now Nova put a question to his creator on the screen.

'Why did they bring the so-called shift-ship so near to us for its maiden failure?'

'To give you a choice. When we fire up the Drive for the jump, the backblast'll fry you. But if you surrender and bring that crate aboard, you'll survive.'

'I'm not in any danger from your Drive.'

'There's no fool like a fibreglass fool. I'll tell you something which may surprise you. I'm glad these people are using my principles for an interesting application. Most don't even believe their beliefs will build to some shattering crescendo. They simply assume in the most mundane manner. This isn't boring is it?'

'If it worked? Yes, it would be, as a matter of fact.'

'Fact. What a quaint term. I gave you the blood of a man, or something like it, but I guess I really did fail – you still don't understand what it is to be human. We journey through life throwing a meaning ahead of us to walk on.'

'Anyone who walks, walks on what's there. The meaning is just a tone we give it. I dare you to walk where there is no path, father.' Nova thought about it. 'Well that's what you're trying, isn't it? I actually would like to see it.'

Baum looked offscreen at something. 'Well, we're

about ready here, Nova. To believe is human.'

'To be told what you believe, is human – these days. I think, father, I'd like to be less human.'

'Why.'

'To be less a slave. Good luck with your experiment.'

'It's not -'

Nova cut off the transmission.

He mused, spinning his nose.

'Your tinpot captain orders you to move off, but only because there'll be nothing to see and we have business on Europa. Obedience is your choice.'

As Nova's cruiser moved off, the battleship's Decree Drive fired up.

Nothing changed, of course – not even Baum's mind. He selected a small tech excuse for the Drive's failure, and everyone immediately set about believing it.

EVERNEMESI

Jeff Lint was told he wrote as if *Moby Dick* had never been published, to which he responded that most people *lived* as if it hadn't. Did Melville think trouble was scarce? Captain Ahab went out of his way to find a whale to cope with but the one time I met a whale it made itself easily available on the beach and we had trouble dealing with its requests – we'd expected it to ask for water or money, but all it said was it wanted to listen to the radio because that was part of its normal routine at this time of day. My hackles were rising after a couple of hours of this. 'Why don't you act like a proper whale and just look at us with your little eye, a tragic thing we don't know how to handle?' But it started discussing the news, and how those jokers in Washington had got us into another oil war. Finally I just walked away, ignoring the shouts of my colleagues. Apparently the others got him back into the water eventually, by rolling him with a bulldozer or something. It must have made a hell of a noise. And that's the story of the whale.

Any real writer will tell you that animals are the main thing standing in the way of the work. Once I was starting a new book and a bison put its head in the window and just stood there, more or less looking at the floor or into a space above it. It seemed perfectly content for the moment - and so was I. But as time passed without anything really changing I realised my day had been taken for ransom. Another time a badger jumped onto the keyboard and started shouting at me. And none of its ideas were fresh or original. Then there was the time a trapdoor opened and I fell into a cellar plagued with rats. As far as I could tell every single one of the thousand or so rats was exactly the same. Again, why the repetition of the same idea? It could be that they were different from each other in some subtle way I didn't understand, but what could it be? Would they begin individually expressing different viewpoints and notions never heard before? Or simply attack me in the most boring way, each rat gnashing in roughly the same manner as its neighbour? I'll leave you to guess which was the case.

But sometimes it's my fault entirely. The incident with the whale left me feeling obscurely ashamed and when the opportunity arose to rescue a jellyfish from the beach and toss it back into the waves, I jumped at the chance. But the jellyfish almost exactly resembled a semi-transparent version of my own face - or perhaps it was just my reflection. I couldn't stop looking at the thing. Someone passing by gave me a glance of disapproval and I felt obliged to pretend I was a principled man. I stood there in the manner of Soviet hero art, but instead of a flag or sledgehammer I held the jellyfish I had found. The problem was that I had to regularly break my stance to dampen the jellyfish in a bowl of water, and this interrupted the heroic monumentalism I was going for. By the time most of the water had been absorbed or generally splashed around, a baffled crowd had gathered and were arguing about what I meant. Finally I turned and hurled the thing into the sea, but people paid more attention to my savage yell than the goodness of the act.

I spent days trying to prove that the creature had survived and was thriving in the surf, but all I found were thousands of eels. The eels were made of soft glass and were almost impossible to see in flowing water. Only their eyes gave them away, and those rare occasions they started singing. And when they sang, they would close their eyes. I told the local authorities about it and they just looked at me like I was mad. I even showed them photographs, which I stuck on the police station wall and pointed to with a stick, but the Chief of Police instantly shouted: '*Get* those things off the wall!' And I had expected to be treated like a saviour.

I didn't leave, but got bored sitting there so I started making a thin wet sound like a burning banana skin. This kept me amused for eleven minutes and then I shouted something in impatience. I think it was 'Oh, god, let it end!' or that kind of thing. Maybe 'God I want to kill everyone!' or like that. Several people looked aside at me like a wall of turbots.

During this whole time with the jellyfish, eels and police, I was supposed to be writing the opening chapter of *LINT*. Remembering this, I left the station and immediately saw a happy dog. From the flapping of its ears I thought the dog was running toward me but I realised it was just tossing its head up and down to send its ears flapping – it was looking eager and aglee having just discovered this crazy trick. It stopped as I approached, and I knelt down, putting my right eye directly against the dog's. *That'll let him know*, I thought – then became aware that the hound was sniggering to itself. 'Ah you're not worth it,' I said aloud, straightening up.

'I am,' the dog whispered, looking up at me. 'And you know it.'

And I thought, *The abyss conceals.*

At home, I looked at the screen. A mistake requires a minimum of two moving parts. A bug like a fingernail tremble-walked along the sill.

Three weeks later I was stumbling through smoke and the flopped bodies of three hundred swans, the sky filling with rejuvenated pteranadons bent on revenge. You take your life in your hands when you write one of mine. Should you look down at your own boots kicking through black coins, or up at the horizon patrolled by lies with bright yellow fins? Watched always by a red frog like a beating heart? The distractions are geometrically infinite, years of it receding. But you can leap over it. Riding on a lion whose jaws want you.

WHISPER

When I get bored I go up to a stranger and spin them to face away from me so I can count the disks in their spinal column. 'Do not fear me,' I whisper, 'I am counting.' Some strangers weep into their hands, some run - some cannot run fast enough to escape me. 'Do not run from me,' I whisper directly into their ears, 'I am counting on you not to run. Do not fear me. I am counting.' Some punch my face and stand over me, breathing hard. When I track them down and appear upon their doorstep I whisper, 'Do not punch me, I will fall. Do not run from me, I am counting on you not to run. Do not fear me, I am counting.' Some call the police and have me arrested and placed in to a prison. When I find them years later and stand at the foot of their bed, I whisper, 'Do not call the police, they will arrest me. Do not punch me, I will fall. Do not run from me, I am counting on you not to run. Do not fear me, I am counting.' Some club me to the floor, bind me with steel cable, set fire to me and roll me into garbage. When I return in their old age, a barely human remnant, I whisper, 'Do not club me to the floor, bind me with steel cable, set fire to me and roll me into garbage, I will be harmed. Do not call the police, they will arrest me. Do not punch me, I will fall. Do not run from me, I am counting on you not to run. Do not fear me, I am counting.' To understand, surely, is to forgive?

THE RETRIAL

Jeff Lint's interpretation of Kafka's *The Trial* was that the guilt felt by K - and depended upon by the state - derives from his having allowed the state to become so powerful in the first place. K therefore ultimately accepts his punishment.

In Lint's story 'The Retrial', K feels no such guilt because he allows no such influence and storms into every circumstance like a berserk Touretter, somehow spanning the most chasmic beartraps by sheer velocity of mischief.

Lint's K is a classic Lintian hero - individual to the point of parallel-dimensionality. In his novel *Jelly Result* Lint would portray the maintenance of oppression by automated human patch-and-repair, those dependent systems simultaneously and constantly preying on the life force of its maintainers. This is Lint's idea of hell and he revels in the hero's disengagement from it. His attempt at an Asimovian short, 'The Robot Who Couldn't Be Bothered', portrays a robot whose apparently faulty inactivity is discovered to be the result of 'eleven million nodes of personal consideration'. The entire second half of the novel *I Am a Centrifuge* is taken up with a volley of justified sarcasm so detailed and complete as to have its own visible lungs and nervous system. The hero in Lint's story 'Bless' awakes one morning to find that he has no tentacles. Alarmed, he dashes out to discover that nobody else has any tentacles either and all claim in bafflement never to have had any. As Michael Hersh has observed, the metaphor points up 'a moral or ethical sensibility which, unheld and unrecognized by anyone else on the planet, is not communicable'. In most Lint stories this sensibility is that of honesty and independent thought.

In 'The Retrial', Joseph K visits the zoo one morning to be greeted by two warders, Franz and Willem, who tell him he's under arrest. He laughs good-naturedly, asking to see their underwear. They refuse, and this lack of reciprocity - their assumption that he must obey their commands while they need not obey his - is what seems to spark K's apparently uncooperative attitude. An Inspector is stood scowling nearby but since no introduction or instruction is given and all is left to some unspoken assumption, K begins to shudder in place like a dodgy steam tank, his convulsions building as though toward some terrible outburst. At the apex his head sags like a bag, splitting to release precisely eleven scorpions on to the ground. K himself collapses like a rotted scarecrow and soon, kicked and scattered by the fleeing crowd, is no longer really in evidence. He is at the court, kicking the outer wall of the Usher's cabin. "'I'm naked", he thought, almost amazed: "First being born, and now this. No trousers for me."' When grabbed by

K, the Usher sees that the complicated epaulets on K's shoulders are actually the skulls of rabbits. He pleads with K to get off, that he has his own troubles, but K is adamant about doing what he sees as his duty. Finally four under-ushers try to pull them both out of the cabin but are foiled. The scene cuts to what appears to be several days later, as the Usher lays inert amid a jumble of steaming wreckage. There is a strange slamming sound as the Usher's eyes start open.

Thus begins a course of what Jean-Marie Guerin has called 'ecstatic disregard' in relation to memo-level fascism: 'Without this undercurrent of beatific irreverence it is impossible to pin down Lint's Joseph K's complete lack of need or desire to become involved with the processes of oppression. It should be noted also that the "berserk stenographer" style in which Lint relates the story is important in allowing these situations to actually appear less philosophically interesting than they are.'

Lint's K tells the story 'Beside the Law', in which a man from the country comes to the door seeking admittance to the Law, but the guard says he can't come in now. So the man constructs a precise replica of the door and locates it beside the first one, placing a sign above it for '$20 a blowjob' and waiting for trade, which is brisk. Finally, when the guard at the first door is about to die, he asks why people stopped coming to his door. 'That door could be profitable only for you,' the man from the country says. 'And now I'm going to close it.'

Like Kafka's K, Lint's has a mind of his own, but unlike that K, he has a breathtaking intuition for the lateral response: a sort of laser-guided effrontery. When asked where he was on a particular evening, K replies: 'Well, I'll tell you - if you have any money?' Outraged, the Magistrate's response is cut short by his perceiving what seems to be a mere sheaf of undulating bacon fibres where K had previously been standing.

Anyone who has actually broken official protocol will know that at best it sends its agents into a sort of contentless whirl which does not have the vibrancy of honest panic, nor even that of genuine surprise - they seem merely to swerve from familar bureaucratic rails onto some of the minor, less used branches of evasion. Nothing is ever changed, admitted or learned. Yet in the world of 'The Retrial' some effect can be had; perhaps by the sheer diagonal intensity of K's responses. Consider the cathedral scene - while you or I might merely windmill our arms and puff our cheeks out a bit, K delivers a roundhouse to the priest by detonating into a perfumed cloud of dandelion seeds and buff-coloured smoke. The priest, who had been 'smiling like a warship' only seconds before, now crouches on the floor like a spider, 'karking and keening' - he seems to have been both deafened and confused by the blast.

Recent critics have suggested that the satirical accesses of Lint heroes are a result of intense tetraneutron activity, supposedly explaining their combination of precision and apparent chaos. Hypercomplex satire operates by applying social rules in the 'wrong' contexts such as those of logic, morality or honesty, and the four-prong tetraneutron cluster (the four neutrons of which will arrive simultaneously if fired at a carbon target) would seem the perfect structure for it - all the more entertainingly so as the phenomena's existence is doubted. If you tweak the laws of physics to allow four neutrons to bind together, all kinds of chaos ensues (*Journal of Physics*, vol 29, L9). It would mean that the mix of elements formed after the big bang was inconsistent with what most people now believe and, even worse, the matter created would be far too heavy for the current model to cope.

The theory stated in Lint's story 'Death by Fred' is that 'sabotage is best accomplished by channeling bad luck'. In Lint, until you're an individual, you're not in contention. This is why Lint could never write about the sort of characters that appeared in other people's books. Almost every scene has a sort of surreal exultation to it.

At the moment his case is due to be heard, K is watching the lions at the zoo, his eyes full of tears. Two men approach and, their arms entwined with his on either side of him, begin to walk him through the city. K begins smiling, the grin seeming to become broader than his face. Finally they arrive at an abandoned quarry. The two men take out a butcher knife and begin passing it to each other in a threatening manner. He is apparently supposed to take it and plunge it into himself. But without aid of the knife a red ace of hearts blooms at his chest and spreads quickly to stain his entire body and head. He has become a pillar of blood in the shape of a man, which soon becomes semi-transparent. It fades until only his Cheshire-cat grin remains, a miniature sunset which whispers echoing as it disappears: 'Like a god!'

VOYAGE OF THE IGUANA

In the course of researching my unpublished novel *Velvet Dogs* I heard tell of an elderly gentleman who had in his possession a collection of ancient ship's journals - first-hand records of the great days of sail – and resolved to seek him out and ask him if he would lend me some money. The hermit-like figure which greeted me in a Bristol attic some months later was nothing if not eccentric, as he sat in a corner stroking a dry fern. 'This is one of my few remaining pleasures,' he explained in a whisper, and embarked upon such a rampant fit of coughing that I feared he would expire then and there; he soon recovered, however, and told me the details of his life until I could barely see. Bringing the conversation around to the subject of finance I established that he had in his possession a full eighty pounds, and offered to invest this sum in porkbelly futures. One of the items he removed while kneeling to search through an old oak chest was a thick, leather-bound volume such as I had originally heard tell in connection with this slavering gentleman. Taking up and leafing through its autumnal pages, I immediately recognised its likely value. At my questioning its authenticity, however, the ancient man took sudden umbrage, producing an antiquated musket the size of a water buffalo. As I took my leave he blew a hole in the roof and a shaft of sunlight burst through, at which the old man hissed and threw an arm across his eyes. A month later I attempted to return the journal and to collect my eighty smackers but found the hermit's house boarded up, and learned from a neighbour that he had been dragged to an asylum hollering that he was inflatable. Thus I inherited the text which is here entitled *Voyage of the Iguana*.

The log relates the events of the most undisciplined sea voyage in maritime history. Captained by a Samuel Light Sebastian in 1808 for the East India Company, it was rarely mentioned with anything less than hollering ire and stabbing daggers. An 1815 *Naval Chronicle* alludes to 'Master Sebastian' in an article entitled 'Damnable Treachery', but this probably refers to a later incident. The maudlin voyage of the *Iguana* surpassed any other for aquatic entropy - Havanans still speak of the 'kennel' which floated into the harbour in 1808, and their name for Sebastian cannot be translated.

It was his first log, though his second voyage as Captain - the first was that of the *Phantom* in 1807, which he boarded as Midshipman. When mutiny broke out and the Captain and Mate were set adrift in a barrel he took over the Captaincy in a daring stroke which apparently involved plying the crew with sixty gallons of rum and then wearing a bonnet so that everyone aboard mistook him for their mother. Bringing the ship into Blackwall Harbour he received a hero's welcome and a commendation from the Board of Control, who in blind gratitude formally promoted him to Captain a year later.

As Captain of the *Iguana* his main occupation seems to be throwing empty bottles at passing Hammerheads, which he constantly asserts are 'sneering' at him. His term is characterised by languid indifference and a startling ignorance of seamanship - he was frequently known to give the order 'Bows full to stern', a manoeuvre which would entail sawing the ship into two equal halves and folding it into a sandwich. A short time into the voyage he seems uncertain as to the ship's destination, cargo (tea probably) or name - the easygoing First Mate Leggahorn voices the opinion that 'if we cannot remember it it cannot be important'. The crew 'discharge pistols' at each other, make parting remarks while leaping overboard, are attacked by cannibals and hallucinate rampantly. Most remarkable is the fact that they never thought seriously to take over command.

Many questions remain unanswered. What was the ship's course? How could it make half the journey without ballast? What was so horrific about the native ritual performed on August 7th that it caused Sebastian and the First Mate to black out? And most intriguingly, where did Sebastian keep his log? - he seems never to be parted from it. Few clues are yielded by maritime records - Sebastian's name seems largely to have been struck out of history. On returning to England in March 1809 he was frantically demoted to 'man without honour abode or employment' and it seems to have been a full two weeks before he was once again at sea, as Captain of a 54-gun store-ship which Lord Cochrane commandeered and deliberately blew up to surprise the enemy.

Steve Aylett

27th May. SSW. Sailed out of Bristol harbour with a fair wind. Introduced myself and First Mate Leggahorn to crew, who responded with mirth. One man stood peeing over rail throughout. Second Mate Forfang interrupted my speech by yelling an obscenity, at which crew erupted into laughter. Morale high.

28th May. SWW. High winds. Leggahorn lost his hat and seven men restrained him from leaping overboard to retrieve it. Remarked to young apprentice Batch that nothing excused such behaviour, at which point all eight men stumbled back and trampled us underfoot.

29th May. SSS. Heavy seas - Mr Byron continually turns his back on wheel and leans laughing at activities of crew as course deviates. Leggahorn and myself forced to separate Forfang and bosun fighting at entrance to saloon - Forfang hammered my head repeatedly against door as big sea came aboard and lifted Leggahorn and bosun on to the fore yard. Everyone swore like the devil. Mr Byron remarks that the incident will provide me with something to tell my grandchildren.

30th May. SSE. Fair sailing again - rain let up, no sea aboard, bosun died down and wind dropped. Forfang lifted me up by the leg and pushed me against the sterncastle, with a mighty yell. All's well.

31st May. SSW. Drenching thunderstorms, big sea aboard, funeral for bosun marred by returns of body. Mizzen-boom sail blown to ribbons. Went to question cook as to hull damage, but he had the gall to say it was not his concern. Spirits raised by Forfang, who is still celebrating yesterday's fair weather. Sent first mate aloft to look for funny clouds.

1st June. SWS. Ship snugged down, lower topsails, fore staysail, reefed fore coarse and spanker. Crew fighting on deck. Leggahorn told us at dinner an amusing story about man who was eaten by a panther. Giving bosun seven lashes for firing musket on deck but wind blew him overboard.

2nd June. NNE. Spoke to Forfang in my cabin about morale, but swinging lantern which struck head upset his mood and he pursued me about the table, until in a position to dash my head upon it, with access of loud laughter. Have determined to indulge in draughts tomorrow. Leggahorn seen hollering obscenities on the topgallant footropes.

3rd June. NNW. Trouble in galley due to lack of food. Stray barrel below burst and flooded passage with rum, at which crew fought to lie down, gurgling and yelling obscenities. Leggahorn and myself strolled deck in coats and seaboots, sat down to play draughts. Pieces vanished instantly upon opening case. Struggle getting back to cabin through men in passage.

4th June. NNS. Ventured above with ship's dog, which flew overboard on being released for exercise. John Tunny tells me through blur of waves that it is a bad start to a voyage when one cannot tell where ship ends and sea begins. Agreed with a laugh, at which he took offence and waded away.

5th June. SSN. Shortage of meat and provisions which cannot be explained. Am in process of checking cargo books. New bosun - Piper. Forfang tripped on the cathead and flew into a rage, breaking his own leg.

6th June. SWE. Provisions underloaded. Gathered crew on deck to inform them but could not make myself heard above the thunder and waves. Forfang hurled heavy barrel at my countenance. Harker continually pees over rail.

7th June. WWN? Leggahorn taught crew hornpipe dance on deck - seven overboard. Spoke to Batch in cabin about his duties as apprentice, but he was knocked out by falling ceiling. News of provisions provoked Berringer to wail 'That's it lads, we're done for - damned to hell one and all.' Could not help but admire his attempts at diplomacy.

8th June. Strolled the deck today, supervised manning of crossjack braces. Parkins and others swore at me through wind and rain. Turtle blown aboard. Hit Leggahorn while laughing on starboard rail. Bad omen.

9th June. Am worried about ship's doctor, who on boarding ship at start of voyage, was suffering from typhoid. Had to retire straightway to rest and nursing by Mate, Leggahorn. Weather still stormy. Batch joined us for dinner - turtle. Flippers had been stolen by certain members of crew, who attached them to their ears and performed demonic ritual. Had those responsible scrub deck, but were washed overboard. Memorial service held, but was washed overboard. All now fastened below save for Harker, who is peeing over rail.

10th June. A glorious morning. Calm sea. Sail repairs going ahead well. Blue skies and fair sailing. Forfang in good spirits, despite broken leg. First mate singing on deck. Ten overboard.

11th June. Fair weather continues. Mr Byron sets his features and lashes himself to the wheel. About midday Forfang punched First Mate Leggahorn, who had been standing in good humour on the poop. Forfang unrepentant. John Tunny tried to heave him overboard, but Forfang knocked him out with lower brace. All's well.

12th June. Had the crew mending sails. Hold taking in water. Took Batch to rail and spoke of the sea. Showed him how to annoy the Hammerheads.

13th June. Spoke to Forfang about his dribbling, at which he took a fragment of plank and attempted to strike me, screaming and foaming as Leggahorn wrestled him out of cabin. Polished my chinaware.

14th June. Bosun devoured by second mate. Laughter.

15th June. Fair weather. Sails and Forfang bellying out.

Position uncertain. Crew either working well, sleeping, or drowned. Exception is Harker, who seems never to cease peeing over rail.

16th June. Berringer calculates that following our present course and allowing for cross-currents our position will be 'the death' of him. While shaving in clear air on deck, Forfang reminded me about the mizen topgallant bunt lines which were severely damaged in storm, and gaining an unsteady grip upon my leg, tried in fits and starts to pitch me over port rail. Making headway in steady wind. Leggahorn at hold ceiling supervising repairs.

17th June. Position still uncertain. Gathered all my charts and instruments together and bundled down to the cook with them, but he was of no aid whatsoever. Stood on forecastle, watching sunset. Perhaps I am becoming a broken man.

18th June. Leggahorn told amusing joke at dinner - pig and trampoline. Will repeat it to Lord Cochrane. Hurled bottles at Hammerheads and watched them becoming annoyed. Gave rat some bread.

19th June. Spoke to sailmaker at work on the poop, and was hit by flying mackerel. Sailmaker, looking up from his work at that moment, collapsed hollering with laughter. Had finally to be carried below and given a whiff of salts.

20th June. Found tiny terrapin on deck. Laughed and laughed. Have determined to nurse it back to health. New bosun - Landis - drowned in his own snot.

21st June. Assembled crew on deck and told them joke - pig and trampoline. One man shouted an obscenity but the others laughed. Repairs still underway.

22nd June. Albatross for dinner. Bad omen.

23rd June. Forfang forced my head through porthole and wrenched at it from other side, with able help from all hands. Cried out loudly for assistance, and Leggahorn appeared in high spirits, eating grapes one by one and attempting to lighten my mood with quips. Onset of darkness put an end to their exertions. All's well.

24th June. Heard more reports of Harker peeing over rail for long hours. Went up on deck and confronted him. He was peeing over rail. 'Listen to me, man, all this peeing over the rail has got to stop,' I told him. He merely looked a little pained and hurt - I went away feeling somewhat ashamed. Cast a glance back and found he was peeing over rail. Suppose he has designs on the Captaincy.

25th June. Alarmed by the change in Batch, the apprentice, who has taken to standing unrobed in entrances. Unresponsive to my offer of an orange, or indeed to anything. Confronted Berringer on deck and suggested that we consult the charts together, to which he replied that I should go below and consult 'the devil'. Forfang turned to me today and yelled piercingly. Appointed new bosun - Parkins - who on hearing news jumped overboard.

26th June. First Mate Leggahorn informs me that crew have taken to eating their trousers. Told him joke about snail and theatre ticket. Laughter.

27th June. Hearing violent shaking of canvas, went forward to see cause. Only Batch prodding it with oar. Crew in low spirits. Attempted jollity by hurling starfish in artful manner, but hit Forfang in face.

28th June. Leggahorn gave swimming lesson off forecastle to Tobias, burly cargo loader, who was taken up by waves and slammed insensible against our bows.

29th June. Went below to visit doctor, who gripped my arm and gasped something about 'damnation'.

30th June. Ship adrift on still water - no wind at all. New bosun - White. Much perturbation caused by Batch standing at rails and grieving that he saw a rhino in the water, and called for hours that crew go to its aid, but none else aboard saw such a hapless beast. Leggahorn and myself questioned cook as to likelihood, but he seemed unable to answer.

1st July. Watched the sneering Hammerheads. Mr Byron unlashed himself from wheel and fell to deck with groan. Leggahorn and myself sat on the quarterdeck, sketching dogs from memory. Batch stood amidships and upended rum-barrel on head, standing in silence thereof a full hour. John Conk mutters about sausages.

2nd July. Bosun yelled 'Green fields - baloo...!' and leapt from the foremast. Memorial service disrupted by Forfang discharging musket at surfacing pilchard.

3rd July. Nobody remembers what we are carrying, and I must confess our destination eludes me. Batch says it may have been coconuts. Harker pees over rail. Leggahorn says if we cannot remember it it cannot be important. John Tunny grasps me by the arm and moves his lips without a sound.

4th July. Had to belay Forfang's order that crew eat their own legs, though crew clearly dismayed at sudden change of plan. Still no wind. Rats uneasy.

5th July. Still no wind. John Conk entertains crew by kicking his own head. Leggahorn makes a cloth effigy of his mother. I stay below, practising mime.

6th July. Investigated hold with lamp. Found dry pickle on shelf. And book filled with pictures of swans. Several upright beams - probably part of ship. Three empty barrels - one so covered in moss that I have installed it in my cabin as a comfortable chair. Leggahorn offered to organise what he termed a 'snot party' in the hold, but I did not question him further.

7th July. Wind picked up. Leggahorn knocked unconscious falling from hammock. Hazlitt fired musket at surfacing blowfish - target exploded with great velocity, blinding him in one eye. New bosun - Fennel - constantly rounds on imaginary attackers and screams of a 'conspiracy'. Crew stare at me through rigging. Rat overboard rescued by Mr Byron.

8th July. Heavy seas. Confronted Berringer on deck and commended him for his skill as a mariner - a remark which provoked him to spit into the wind and yell inaudibly through the crash of the waves, holding up a jellyfish and tearing it in half and jabbing a finger at my chest. Told him to keep up the good work, and went to supervise manning of braces.

9th July. After brief survey it seems nobody remembers name of ship. Searched cabin books unsuccessfully for reference. Batch says it may have been *Coconuts*. Big sea aboard. Nobody on deck save for Harker peeing over rail. Ventured above in coats and seaboots, confronted him at rail. Bellowed over the storm that he should go below. He replied that the men would not approve of his peeing down there. I suggested with a mighty yell that he might cease peeing, but his expression as he turned to me was disconcertingly blank.

10th July. Heavy seas. Lowered Forfang over side to read name of ship. Hauled up claiming to have seen a bison. Three men overboard. Forfang informs us with a gasp of exhaustion that he was never taught to read.

11th July. Damage done to navigational equipment by Leggahorn with sledgehammer during storm. Some charts soaked in cabin spillage, others eaten for dinner by Leggahorn, second mate and myself. Story about broken fruit - how we roared!

12th July. Bosun began rounding on himself and careering across the quarterdeck, punching his own nose. Leggahorn told him to simmer down but he started up again in the afternoon, juddering amidships and pitching over rail. Memorial service disrupted when Forfang hollered from the ranks that the hull was covered in edible crustacea and all hands leapt overboard.

13th July. Fair weather today. Interrupted Berringer as he was hauling on main braces. Halting his oaths in mid-volley he turned to me and spat in recognition.

Asked him how long he had been a mariner, to which he replied twenty-five 'bloodthirsty' years, and added 'in God's name' that he would not be here today were it not for the charity of my 'black and empty' heart. I thanked him and he struck my countenance, at which crew's spirits revived and they struck up a shanty, dancing lustily on deck. Twenty overboard.

14th July. Sentenced Batch to fifty lashes for tugging on lantern. Piped all hands amidships to witness punishment, but were washed overboard. Forfang and I caught in the mizen braces, where waves soon rendered us senseless. Leggahorn remained below, smoking my pipe and reading Smollett.

15th July. Hazlitt fired harpoon at surfacing anchovy - complains that loss of eye affects his aim. Became offended at my suggestion that he choose a larger target. I stayed in cabin for the rest of day, trying to remember my name.

16th July. Issued pay today, with lukewarm response from crew - many looked blankly at money without recognition, and some, after brief examination, swallowed it down. Bad omen.

17th July. Having a fair wind, set our foresail and ran aground with a sound which Leggahorn compared to 'the shout of a moose' - indeed he blocked the passageway for several moments laughing uproariously as I tried to go above. Found that most of crew on deck were similarly occupied, bent double and hollering with mirth despite damage to vessel. Black outcrop towered over sails and big sea spumed out of the breakers. Harker yelled while peeing over rail that the only individual capable of mending that kind of damage was the god of hellfire. Leggahorn put a comforting hand on my shoulder and was washed overboard. Consulted cook, who held up biscuit and ranted, pointing at it and himself with loud assertions. Taking on water - crew disheartened at having to sleep in rigging.

18th July. Myself, Leggahorn and John Tunny entered cargo hold and rowed across in barrels to inspect hull damage. Leggahorn held lantern under visage and contorted his countenance. Informed him of the graveness of our careers. Laughter. Outcrop intruded through gash in hull - John Tunny suggested we keep it for ballast. He and Mr Byron created powder keg ignited with muskets, setting sails alight and ship adrift. Bows full to stern. Spider in cabin!

19th July. Navigating shores of this dark isle hindered by list of vessel to starboard. Concerned for crew, who are so long at sea that they seem unaware of land's significance. Hazlitt voiced the uncertain opinion that it was some sort of pudding. Mr Byron states openly that he would like to have the wheel 'covered in wool'. Weather calm and warm. Gave Leggahorn fifty lashes for molesting figurehead.

20th July. Came upon palmy bay and resolved to go ashore. Commanded Mr Byron to let go the anchor, but he remained unmoved. Took the efforts of eight men to wrestle it from him, provoking his tears. Told him to get a grip on himself. Left him aboard with Harker. Rowing out, saw that ship was called *The Iguana.* Crew disconcerted. On landing, crew ignored my instructions on unloading of provisions and ran hollering into the jungle. I camp alone this night under tree. Used lamp to signal ship that all is well.

21st July. Crew came bellowing out of the jungle covered in mud. Leggahorn reported that he had discovered something of importance, then showed me his belly and ran away. Hazlitt walked laughing down the beach, arms akimbo and a melon balanced on his head. John Conk passed by, kneeing himself in the groin. Forfang beat the life out of me with an oar and told of a crocodile encountered in jungle. Spoke alarmingly of his attempts to 'embrace' it, an enterprise thwarted by the depths of an interceding stream. Hazlitt repeatedly fired musket at sand and broke into hysterical laughter. Leggahorn told him to speak his mind, then showed him his belly and ran away. Forfang missing in jungle. Crew buried me and fell into drunken stupor.

22nd July. Crew amused themselves with shooting at coconuts into which were carved my own features. Excused myself and went for a brisk swim.

23rd July. Savages attacked as I attempted to entertain crew with impersonation of hen - took us prisoner and broke our spirit by pouring rum into the sea. Leggahorn screams incessantly. John Conk shakes like a patient of Bedlam. Ordered Berringer to communicate our friendly regards to the savages, at which he grasped the arm of one and began to sob openly. Hazlitt cheerily remarks upon our good fortune at not being washed into sea when we were vomiting earlier.

24th July. Savages tied us down and clubbed what Berringer translated as 'the living bloody daylights' out of us with branches. Batch tells us about Moses and then rouses indignation by breaking into laughter. Berringer has identified our location as 'the devil's own continent' and indeed there are countless snakes.

25th July. Savages clubbed us again, wearing colourful masks today and pausing only briefly to answer my enquiries. Berringer said that their masks were 'Gali-masks' and that they referred to the snakes as 'Bo-Mambas', which are apparently capable of 'sucking the ruddy life out of the lot of us'. Have determined to take on the responsibility of Batch's education - informed me today that he had forgotten the meaning of the word 'happiness'.

26th July. Savages clubbed us again today. I advised Berringer to comb his beard. His snarled, spitting response was inaudible above the screaming of his crewmates.

27th July. Savages stated today while clubbing us that it was their intention to 'bake' us and dine 'laughing' upon our scorched frames. Leggahorn stares at me. Morale low.

28th July. Expended arduous thought on how to deal with savages. Leggahorn suggests I promote them to bosun. Conferred with cook, who responded with loud access of sobbing. Savages count our limbs and draw calculations in sand, chattering with easy laughter and rupturing tree-trunks with their bare hands.

29th July. Savages scattered by crocodile which came thrashing out of the jungle and up to Berringer, biting his arm and lying beside us with a leer. Our screams rose immediately in pitch but this seemed only to increase its amusement. Forfang appeared and we begged him to loose our bonds, which he accomplished by firing among us with a musket. John Conk fainted. The rest of us screamed with such abandon that the savages ran to our aid, scattering again under Forfang's fire. Untied, a relieved Leggahorn thanked Forfang with a gasp of exhaustion and knocked him senseless with a rock.

30th July. Surveyed ship with spyglass. Saw Harker, peeing over rail. Signalled with musket that all is well. Mr Byron fired back, wounding Hazlitt and sending crew hollering into jungle. Forfang takes crocodile on lead during exploration. Weary round-robin naming of reptile, during which I vote heartily for Jonathan - crew spat into fire and agreed on 'Darly'. John Tunny added with a sneer that it was probably just some animal 'made of leather'. It is good to see them taking an interest.

31st July. Instructed several of crew as to difference between ferns and coconuts, with orders to load the ship with coconuts and freshwater. Myself, Leggahorn and others penetrated deep into the jungle, exploring the area where Forfang 'had his frenzy', Hazlitt 'carved a chimp' and Leggahorn apparently 'talked for hours about steam'. Soon, however, we were in unexplored territory and John Conk began whining and repeatedly blowing his nose. Discovered many temples dedicated to the worship of snakes, gazelle and other insects. Our guide, a savage whom Berringer refers to as 'Death', told us that many rituals took place here, including one during which a toad was pulverised by a heavy stone mallet, sacrificed to the infernal fury of the god Rakata, and examined. Crew prayed before a few stone images and left earrings, trousers and such as tribute. Returned to find ship filled with ferns. Shall remain another day.

1st August. Gathered coconuts and spoke of our adventures. Berringer joked that he was a wanted man and showed us a dagger, claiming that it was 'the very one'. Batch surprised us all by strangling a trout. Forfang tried to ride on Darly's back but kept dismounting in a hurry. Leggahorn and I exchanged jokes about ash - how we roared!

2nd August. Crew gathered coconuts and taught Death a hornpipe dance. Results were so unnerving that everyone begged his assurance that he would not repeat it. Berringer gripped my arm and brandished a fistful of seaweed at me with sundry assertions. Told him to 'simmer down'. Consulted cook as to sailing conditions, at which he retreated deep into jungle. Dawson entertained us with a song about bats. John Conk kept time by clubbing his own head. Hazlitt began to rant and drowned his accordion. All's well.

3rd August. Gave John Tunny fifty lashes for raping a dove. Leggahorn said he was tired of supervising loading of coconuts and ran around camp showing everyone his belly. Forfang remarked rampantly upon my neglect in failing to converse with crocodile, and stood over me watching my initial efforts. Having knelt and bid the beast Good-day I could not establish as to whether it was well and Forfang kicked me away with a roar.

Berringer told us of his time at Clerkenwell. Laughter.

4th August. Leggahorn, Hazlitt and myself went to waterfall in jungle. Hazlitt claimed a carp was smiling at him. Gathered a few coconuts. In our absence Forfang promoted Amberley to bosun and maimed him with a marlin's nose. Funeral service disrupted when Death broke from the ranks and embarked upon a hornpipe dance.

5th August. Fogg approached me with a belt. I departed to a sandbank where crew were burning flags. Hazlitt threw in a crab which exploded with such a deafening report that the savages ran to our aid, careering back into the jungle under a volley of muskets. Crew hollered a shanty, each verse of which ended 'Kill the Captain for his trousers'. John Conk kept time by stabbing himself repeatedly in the back and Death, though unsure at first, soon picked up a few words. All's well.

6th August. Cook came juddering out of the jungle yelling that every animal in the world was after him - I was just telling him to have a shave when a bleak-featured panther peered through the leaves and proceeded to pounce amid the crew, who awoke and began discharging muskets at each other, tearing their trousers from the mouths of tigers and bellowing obscenities - I know not fully the number of beasts which pursued us from the beach but a dozen cats of the sneering variety swam alongside our landing-boat, from which we hurled coconuts and volleys of inventive abuse. Crew boarded ship and stumbled hollering amid coconuts, punching each other and pitching overboard. Told Harker that all was well and that we were underway. Peeing over rail, he relayed the order to Mr Byron, who unlashed himself from the wheel and collapsed with groan into coconuts. Lion conveyed aboard clasped to anchor - bit Hazlitt on the arm and stumbled amid coconuts as sails bellied out and we moved off, low in water and overrun with deadly jungle cats. Barricaded door of cabin with coconuts and settled down to pipe and Smollett. Crew say goodnight to one-another and fall asleep lashed to rigging.

7th August. We are safely escaped from the island and no man has suffered disease, save for ship's doctor, who as a result of venturing on deck has contracted malaria. Cook still a little feverish this morning but when I sat aside his bunk and enquired as to our coordinates he suddenly revived, strangling empty air and shrieking with laughter. Gave him a coconut and told him to rest. Forfang wrestles lions on deck. John Conk apparently complains that Darly is lashed to rigging too close to him, and asks to be moved. Crew jeer. Leggahorn and myself have lunch with Death, who tries to describe native ritual and resorts to demonstration, causing Leggahorn and I to black out. Leopard in the bulkhead.

8th August. Three lions trapped in saloon - tempted in by barrel of coconut milk. Berringer locked door laughing and swallowed key, halting in mid-holler and gasping for medical assistance. Leggahorn carried doctor on deck and all hands leapt overboard.

9th August. At dinner Leggahorn made as though to expound a theory as to where we are, and breaking into laughter concluded 'At sea'. Just then Berringer entered and, guessing at what had been discussed, drove Leggahorn's head thirty times against the table, leaving him wild-haired and unresponsive. Saw Darly, whom I still secretly address as Jonathan, dancing today.

10th August. Forfang wrestled two lions and a leopard into landing-boat, setting them adrift. John Tunny remarked indignantly that they weren't even rowing. Told him to simmer down. Crew unlash themselves from rigging and climb down with easy laughter and conversation. I slap Forfang on the back and awake on the wheel box. All's well.

11th August. Heat very strong today. Leggahorn

resourceful in organising network of gangplanks over coconuts on deck. Crew burn a few flags. Forfang gave Darly a kick in the belly for snagging his trousers. Darly made gurgling sounds in throat and thrashed his tail, knocking over buckets. He's not all there, if you seek my opinion.

12th August. Hot sun. Sea calm. Batch teaches Death to foam at the mouth. Death quickly becoming one of the crew. I walk on deck, laughing about coconuts. Crew glare at me, unmoved. I remark aloud that we shall not lack for food, and go swiftly below as Berringer stands.

13th August. Hot again - no wind. Ship low in still water. Threw a few coconuts at the Hammerheads. Death joined me at rail demonstrating new skill - commended him and spoke of the sea. Showed him the sneering Hammerheads. Crew hack out strips of canvas and rig up hammocks on deck. Some make a man out of coconut shells, naming it Old Shaky. I go below and look at pictures of greyhounds.

14th August. Still no wind. Crew awoke complaining of bad dreams and visitations from the dead. I went before crew with the conviction that those who are dead remain so. John Tunny belligerently asserted that he possessed the ruddiest bum on the high seas - I retreated with the repeated assurance that I believed him.

15th August. Still no wind. Mr Byron lashed himself to wheel hollering 'It's a typhoon lads - biggest I've ever seen' until Forfang knocked him senseless. Went and thanked him on behalf of the men and awoke near the cathead. John Conk struck up a shanty about bloody murder, keeping time by clubbing himself over the head with an oar. Batch confers aloud with his grandfather. I go below and thoughtfully devour coconuts.

16th August. No wind. Spoke to Fogg at rail, commending him for his steady service. He did not regard me but whispered urgently for silence so that he could 'hear the actors speaking'. I looked out to sea, but could perceive nothing but green fields. Advised him to go below and rest but he pushed me aside yelling that he had paid for this balcony and 'on t'balcony I'll stay!'

17th August. Berringer entered cabin with cutlass today and made remarks. Told him I would give them consideration, at which he left hollering with laughter. I consult with my mother and she tells me to 'simmer down'.

18th August. I stroll on deck, ducking under hammocks. Leggahorn reports a 'large, angry face' off the starboard bow and I respond with hilarity. Batch grows a mushroom in his hat. I roll up a chart and, striding, shout through it from the sterncastle that coconuts are the stuff of life. Crew strike up a shanty and dance on deck, pointing in amazement at empty air. I ascend to crow's nest and set light to my trousers, dropping them into sea like burning bird. New bosun - Old Shaky. Forfang and Death ensnare a magistrate. I go below, laughing.

19th August. Leggahorn and I attempt to sit Darly at table but he writhes off and away. Finally achieved by tying him in chair with length of cable about belly. Seated facing away from cabin door, turned to leer at John Conk who entered heartily and fainted. Laughter.

20th August. Carved miniature pelican from coconut today. Spoke to Harker as he was peeing over rail - told me it was 'a voyage and a half, this one' and laughed himself scarlet. Leggahorn and I spend the afternoon hallucinating. Sun sets through tattered sails as Berringer shoots a gull. All's well.

21st August. Leggahorn and I hallucinate all morning, and then take Death aside to teach him rules of pontoon. Crew gather round, placing bets, but to everyone's alarm Death wins and begins dancing his joy - eight men fall unconscious and two leap overboard. Four strong men tie him to mast and forbid him to participate in any such game. He seems confused though eager to comply.

22nd August. Watched basking sharks at rail. Remarked to Mr Byron that it were good to spend one's life doing nought but drifting around with one's mouth agape, to which he agreed and added that he would do the same were he in my position. In the afternoon, ship overrun with pirates who fastened crew below at sabre-point and set fire to Old Shaky. Complimented the Captain on his colourful garments. Captain said his name was Murder and, inspecting with a frown the deck arrangement of planks and coconuts, asked me mine. I could not recall it and, gasping with laughter, told him so, at which he ceased his inspection and regarded me with raised eyebrows. I am to spend this night lashed to the flying jib, which Captain Murder says might refresh my memory.

23rd August. Strode the deck with Captain Murder. Offered him a coconut, which he knocked to the deck with the others. Told him I run a tight ship, at which he roared with laughter and said he admired a man with a sense of humour, and that he intended to take my ship and kill myself and the crew. Became indignant at my flushed hilarity. Murder's mate came slamming up through the hatch snarling 'Calenture, Captain - sunstroke - savage foamin' at the gob' and offered his opinion that 'the ship's cursed sir - all barkin' mad as the ides o' march - coconuts everywhere'. At that another dog of fortune burst out of the aft hatch bellowing 'Crocodile eatin' soup at the Captain's table'. Captain swore that he would find a decent meal aboard if it killed him. Hacked his way into saloon and was eaten by three lions. I climb rigging and watch pirates pursued overboard by lions and vessel uncoupling in alarm, moving off with man-eaters roaring on deck. I eat coconuts and watch their retreat, laughing.

24th August. Crew refuse to come above, hollering that all manner of misery occurs on deck. Leggahorn and myself attempted to negotiate but reasoning marred by sudden appearance on deck of Forfang, who fired musket into darkness - their response was one of screams and abuse. With uncommon bravery, Leggahorn prods Forfang's arm and leaps overboard. Cook has locked himself in galley shouting about 'persecution' and smashing his equipment. Darly looked at me today, with his big eye.

25th August. Land sighted - crew erupt above punching each other senseless and straining at the rail. All voiced aloud their notions - 'Cadiz! Tobago! Benidorm! The Cape! Purgatory!' - as town and port became visible. Mr Byron lashed himself to wheel and bade the world farewell. John Tunny became frantic and wondered aloud if we should hoist a flag. Nobody could remember. Drifted near to harbour and set off hollering in landing boats. At wall crew pushed past me as I stood on steps speaking of courtesy and caution, and dashed bellowing into town. Foreigner asked me if I was English - embraced me - asked me into tavern. Told me I was in Havana, at which I took up a brace of pistols and threatened every man present. Backed out blasting away with both hands and bumped into old friend, Burdett, who greeted me with delight and invited me into tavern. Occupants shrieked and ran as I re-entered, and Burdett poured wine and told me of recent events - treaty with Spain, no more killing of Spaniards for us and so on. Told him of damage to ship, eating of charts, arrival of Darly, Death, Old Shaky and my mother, and of many other events which had occurred during the voyage, at which he was aghast. I said that stranger things happen at sea, to which he replied with uncommon emphasis that this was not the case. Forfang entered with Darly on chain and I shouted goodbye to Burdett as he left. Forfang has left me Darly to care for and I am to attempt slumber at an inn this night.

26th August. Took Darly for skitter through town this morning - looked for crew. Saw many citizens who turned and ran. Saw Harker at harbour wall, peeing over rail. Passing ladies disturbed at view. I went and spoke with him, suggesting he attend to his toilet elsewhere. 'I would,' he laughed, 'if I 'ad one!' Continued to pee over rail, and soon seemed unaware of my presence. Entered rowdy tavern. Chained Darly to banister. Met woman who threw herself onto my lap from other side of the room. On the way upstairs thought I saw Berringer's arm in crowd, but as I drew near it punched me senseless. This night I am indisposed in house filled with draperies.

27th August. Scarlet Bella and myself walk Darly through town - look for crew. Bella remarks on man peeing over rail. Laughter. Surprised to see Captain Murder's mate with arm in sling – became enraged when I asked what had happened. Scarlet Bella punched him in the nose and we moved on. Taught Darly to stagger short distance on hind legs - how we roared!

28th August. Spent the day in bed, writing, carving dogs from driftwood and singing dirges. Received a visit from Murder's mate, who made a remark and forced a scrap of paper into my hand, leaving with a slam. Unwrapped it but none the wiser - message obscured by great spot of spilt ink. Folded paper into tiny boat which sank in basin.

29th August. Walked out with Scarlet Bella - witnessed Harker being placed under arrest. Interceded on his behalf and was taken to fort in chains. Cuban officer circled me and became bellicose - criticised my ears, asked me my name. Explained to him that I could not recall this information. Slammed his fist on desk and prodded rampantly at statement, demanding a signature. Told him to find a man called Burdett who would probably know my name. Officer said he had no time to waste and told me to sign with a cross. This I did, scribbling above it a rudimentary order promoting him to bosun. As he took it wall exploded with French cannonball and buried him in rubble. I search dungeon, shooting guards and flicking spiders from my apparel. Find Harker and rest of crew, who tell me they have been arrested for witchcraft. Escape to woodland, where by light of campfire Death entertains us with impression of gasping mackerel.

30th August. Hazlitt says we should go to the harbour dressed as dogs. Rest of crew disagree, claiming that beagles would be more appropriate. Death asks 'What are beagles' and after startled thought, crew decline to reply. Berringer goes out to kill a bear but returns with some weeds which John Tunny adds to a stew. After eating, everyone blacks out and are finally awoken only by heavy thunderstorm. Mr Byron holds wet finger to wind and nods with a smile. John Conk begins shrieking.

31st August. We wander aboardship at four in morning. Berringer grips me by the arm and claims through clenched teeth that he is 'exhausted'. John Conk has gone bananas and believes the world is run by a bear playing the trumpet. Sea stormy. At noon three ships appear in pursuit, bringing down our crossjack with cannonfire. I tell Berringer to change his shirt. He comes at me with axe but Leggahorn intercedes, punching my face. Fire amidships. I rush to consult with cook but he is chopping onions. We take another hit and ship water. New bosun - Glasby. Forfang attempts to wrap me in burning canvas. I tell Harker that all is well. Crew celebrate in final moments and fire Glasby from cannon, taking out mainsail of leading ship. Leggahorn remarks amid renewed jubilation that the *Iguana* has no cannons aboard, and that we must be aboard someone else's ship. Crew cease cheering. Forfang makes a remark and fires cannon, sinking *Iguana* with all hands. Crew begin fighting on deck, vaulting over fallen masts and choking each other against the rails. Big seas aboard. I announce my plans to marry. Mr Byron leans back on wheel and chuckles at the progress of his career. John Conk staggers out of the spray holding a fern. We founder on reef and leap into the tempest. Bad omen.

1st September. Spent morning on beach chatting with crew who sit sobbing among rockpools. Announced that it seemed voyage was at an end, that they had performed admirably and I would welcome the chance to sail with them again. Berringer took his hands from his face and, after a pause, lunged at me with animal yell. A flushed Forfang interceded brandishing oar and I awoke on empty beach. Spent a few hours wandering beach looking for driftwood and colourful shells. Found urchin with black eyes. Wear it on my head in rain and start back to England, where I am to present my report.

THE MAN WHOSE HEAD EXPANDED

Brank Osmen's head parted the city in slow surging waves, immense clouds of powdered glass and concrete getting in his eyes. Not too shabby, but more than he bargained for. As his forehead barged twenty blocks of offices and hotels into the river, he knew the truth makes no exceptions.

Headgloves had become popular when plastic surgery was found to be insufficient. Twitches of human expression would sometimes disarrange and disturb the desired blandness – headgloves avoided this problem by being entirely artificial, a whole-head mask. These became thicker over the years, incorporating embedded nano servo-motors to replicate certain select expressions. People could buy celebrity heads, the deader the eyes the higher the price. The real head of a headglove wearer had to be surgically shrunken to roughly the size of a potato. People wore the headglove their whole lives, their real head shrivelled and forgotten. Some, rich only in money, had their actual head dwindled to the size of a maggot.

The Contraflow Revolutionary Army fought alone, without any lies to help them. Their enemy seemed a weak one, a people who were helpless without disguise and feared honesty like fire. Contraflow favoured girls who exploded out of nowhere with huge tiger smiles, faces of a thousand muscles and two-handled gullwing sedan guns with retro Gatling drums the size of turnstiles. The media's misinterpretation prerogative named them the Nobhead Liberation Army and Brank liked this so much he changed the name officially, laughing the big laugh.

You could tell who was under a mask - smiles didn't reach the eyes, the eyes were false and rain bounced off. Dr Buck's compound, administered by intravenous dart, reversed the head-shrinkage process and the public got their first view of this when a chat-show host's outer head spatted suddenly like a snipered melon, crumbling open to make way for a swelling grey abomination. His real head, which hadn't seen the light of day for forty years, squalled like a child against a dark caul of mould and steaming slime, several cockroaches darting to escape the sudden exposure. Overnight the Nobhead Liberation Army became oppression excuse number one. The authorities asserted that the assaults on headgloves were not activated by a desire to dispose of headgloves: why would anyone? Knowing that a crime investigation was doomed if the motive was so strenuously denied, Brank felt safe.

The Army's headquarters was upstairs from an old chapel fronted by relay monks who dispensed ominous looks to entrants and clasped precaution razors between their prayhands. The night of his weekly broadcast

Brank made the sign of the Errorverse and entered. Not for him an imprecise, amateur apocalypse open to interpretation. Upstairs he passed a rack of carbines and the modified jacuzzi in which several gallons of Dr Buck's incendiary antidote swirled, enough for a city.

Brank loved how much people hated his adolescent doorframe sermonising and so did a lot of other people. A thriving trade had begun in the sound files. He sat at the broadcast desk now and gathered his thoughts, feeling as useless as a hen on a garbage island. Usually he couldn't wait to finish one insult to the populace before beginning the next. He looked up at the skylight roof, and the striplamp swaying on its chain like a bit of sky come loose. Man was he one fried monkey.

Opening the mike, he began. 'This is the Nobhead Liberation Army. You've heard me say that part of enlightenment is knowing when you're being ripped off. Regret is a rope at the other end of which is a younger version of you, all full of beans and acting like a moron. It's not rebellion if they just sold it to you. The opposite of revolution is a script. But when the time comes to realise this, you continue replacing hours with the same hours. You select only from those options presented you by other people and so occupy a lifelong abyss of misdirection. You've been shafted, so what the hell are you grinning at?

'If people truly don't return from the dead, then humanity is constantly passing out of the world and something is being lost - yet there are still bodies and bodies and bodies, moving and talking. Does this explain the increasing blandness, the diminishing thought, the dead eyes? What is passing out of the world, and not returning, is spirit. At what point did street bribes stop paying cops to leave off criminals and begin paying cops to leave off victims? Such trickling transitions are silent as sap. Non-totalitarian governments exist because some populaces are naturally servile or distractible enough not to require a totalitarian one. This one has taken misdirection to intergalactic extremes. Even our tyrants are mostly ornamental. And the headglove is a godsend to this evasion, a mask incapable of anger, doubt, appetite or intelligent scorn, nor the freedom of being an ugly, honest cunt. The new flesh, bright zombie, going one younger. Moods without weather. And the utter sadness of generations not knowing what they've betrayed. Born into this artificiality with no intervening stages, they walk through life as if they have an appointment with their own ghost, a blameless blank crippled by appearances, living a philosophy which has its sensations only in imitation. They're so timid of their own skin that they live like a spirit departing or never present, immaculately inauthentic. They're the dead merely held in reserve.

'But things are more interesting than that. Earlier today I trod on a spider and it made a sound like the pip of an automatic car lock. *Now* tell me this world's not a weird one.

'If you tape the average man's mouth shut he'll lie through his nose. That's undisputed. But we have to ask, what will be the last words spoken on this planet? Concrete cannot complete the universe. The derelict society glitters, celebratory with weakness. Facts are acknowledged only when the events they relate to are far in the past and safely irrelevant. Rare outbreaks of commonsense are stifled and ignored by the media, never heard of. Fatuous influences shrug off the brain for reasons of balance. Warnings of catastrophe are dismissed as mere "warnings of catastrophe" but soon the little patronised problems of chance will be lethal. I await the brave dismay of the honest. Love has the innards of grief.

'Careful: a uniform is a dice. The Nobhead Liberation

Army is slandered but who among you has witnessed a more reasonable frenzy than ours? Who has not experienced the desire to tear off his own face in the midst of society's bullshit? Don't decorate my name with importance. You can't name the saints of true atrophy – the label slips amid our rotting flesh. Irrational perspectives decide the angle of our wounds. We will crash your mind and serve a feast of discouragement. You can tame the loops out of my head when I'm fucking dead. We won't succeed, finally. But after all, what's the point of being doomed in a *variety* of ways?

'Riddle me this: who are you? It's hard to see a system of which you are part. It's hard to see your own eyes. You pay to make fools of yourselves. To hear your own veins drying up. Don't mistake intensity for hostility, mate - some people have things to do. You're a bloodless, clueless wanker and you think you're great - and that's why I get fundamentally disappointed.'

A blare of noise interrupted him, a helicopter above the skylight. 'Put it down, put it down!' came a cry through a loudhailer. 'Desist!'

'How are you spelling that?' Brank yelled, pulling his Daewoo only to sling it away at the end of the motion, all strength gone from his arm – the gun clattered into a corner. His shoulder was bleeding and skylight glass powdered the floor like sugar. There were booming shots from downstairs and as he reached for one of the gullwings a soldier entered. Brank swung and two rashers of uniform flew in different directions.

Then something slapped him in the head. The hot wind from it surprised him. Blood looped out behind him, hitting the wall. It was a graffiti exclaiming 'O'. He'd known he'd end this enterprise utterly licked against a drystone wall, shot-up and bucking in dust, but now it was happening he felt as dumb as an adult in a teacup ride. To be insulted by these fascists was so degrading.

Blood hanging out of his face, he fell backward into Buck's vat.

Feeling squirly, he could still see cloud above the skylight roof. It seemed to be getting closer. Then the window frames were pressing against his face like a griddle. They burst outward and he continued to swell, his head tilting aside so he could see the neighbourhood getting smaller. His head was expanding like a slow bomb, his body a useless doll beneath it. The house began to crumple, dust exploding down the surrounding streets. He felt like hell and tried screaming the fact. Confronted with a massive head momentarily capable of opinion, the authorities were unprepared. Brank was dilating across districts, his head a confusion ball of white and pink fat arching through a spritzed halo of bloodcloud. Power lines spanged, fizzing out. Upheaval edges powdered to rubble. He was making good on his promise to replace glamour with swampy death, to the extent that he was now breaking through a bridge as a train shot up his nose. *Of all the ways I expected to die*, he thought, *this seemed the least likely.* The train passengers were having similar thoughts. Sonic booms shattered windows as tectonic skull plates changed position.

Beyond a certain reach he began losing integrity. Dilating blood vessels tore and brain canals broke. Veins whipped open, hosing the town and tangling with spires. An eye burst like a water-bomb. A tumbling onward wall of cortex was rolling through its own pink rain, proportions stretching, blasting through whole blocks before exploding finally and washing a cascade of wreckage through the tilted city. His last thought was, *To live past hope, like walking into thin air ...*

A slow-motion shower of shredded brainweb like cotton candy floated down on the ruins. Nerve netting stretched between bridges and towers. Pink scum foamed the river. Seagulls picked at the tangle of disease-ridden flesh in yellow liquid. Streets were clogged with dark, hardened gore. The decade-long task began of clearing the slurried headflesh and dismantling the titanic skull which, rested on its side, was almost a mile tall from cheekbone to cheekbone.

Even dismantled it was inconvenient. As in any conflict, false motives had to be set in place. But with this strange episode, invention failed. Humanity had to use time to evade it, a desperate measure. So, inevitably, Brank was canonized. Once an idea has become universally accepted, it's easily ignored.

GRACELAND

In what has been described as a 'stupid bid for attention', Thomas Sumpter, an injection-moulding technician from Dayton, Ohio, released an undernourished leopard into Elvis Presley's Graceland mansion on Saturday. The animal sprang onto the top of a cupboard and watched anxious visitors without saying anything. Apparently sensing that the animal had no intention of mauling anyone at the mansion, Sumpter attempted to entice the leopard from its perch by holding up some chewing gum and making a sound like a cartoon fish. The leopard pounced on Sumpter and became snagged on his garish shirt, tearing itself free with only minor injury to Sumpter's chest. Security staff from Memphis Zoo and Aquarium cornered the big cat in the media room, where it had fallen asleep. When they fired ten tranquillizer rounds into the beast, it awoke in surprise and attacked both men, injuring George Harrod, 38, and Terry Heem, 26. Sumpter finally spoke to the leopard in a whisper and he and the cat left by a rear entrance. Onlookers claim that Sumpter merely whispered to the carnivore that he had become bored with the escapade and that it was time to go. When traced to his Dayton home on Sunday, Sumpter expressed bewilderment at accounts of his antics and claimed that he had not left his home for three days. Doctors have found no wounds on his torso and there was no evidence at Sumpter's home to suggest the care or maintenance of a leopard or similar animal. Injured zoo employee Terry Heem stated on Sunday that he was 'angry and flushed'. Family and friends of his colleague George Harrod told news media that Harrod was 'beaming' and talking like a child. The leopard may still be at large.

CABELL'S NEW SINS
a one-act play

Flames climb the rear of the stage, all is flushed a fierce red and strange convulsing shadows freak the walls - grotesque figures are glimpsed onstage.

CONSCIENCE (a Burroughsian universal voice, casual & laconic): To those with fully-functioning senses the planet Earth is already a living hell and to such folk the prohibitions of those who claim to be in authority come across as absurd at best, drowned out as they are by the high-frequency roar of hypocrisies too extreme to process. Most aware people dream of living a mere few instants of peace, away from the hysterical admonitions of neighbour, god and government. The sins listed are uninventive and boring, and the constant assumption that people are aching to commit them seems designed to insult the human imagination. Consider the case of Lord Cabell, one of the most inconvenient of the fifty-seven rakes of Regency England.

(The flames have died down, normal lighting takes over and the shadows on the rear wall recede - the figures onstage are a bunch of posh Regency types in a large well-appointed drawing room, drinking and being urbane.)

LORD HARKEN: Congratulations on the new poetry, Cabell - everyone's jabbering about its relevance to you alone.

LORD CABELL: Then they understand it - I'm gratified.

HARKEN: This is my wife, the Lady Harken. And allow me also to introduce the Archbishop Strauss. Still managing to be surprised repeatedly by the same thing, padre? I'd like to know how you do it - you're a marvel!

ARCHBISHOP STRAUSS (dubious): Thank you.

HARKEN: This is the poet Lord Cabell. Keeps his morals in an eye-dropper. Author of *Childe Shrub's Adulterous Schedule.*

CABELL (bored): Here I stand, my epidermis flavourless.

STRAUSS: If you live by the same philosophy as your literary protagonist, you will find your arguments derailed by a fiery abyss. A man should perform congress only with his wife.

CABELL: Sex with his wife. Isn't that incest?

STRAUSS: Thou shall not commit adultery, Lord Cabell.

CABELL: Not a very interesting prediction. Am I meant to be tempted to alter it by battling fate?

HARKEN: What is it Shrub says about fate? 'How many deaths are in the lion, awaiting distribution?'

CABELL (uninterested): So, my ink is immoral. Poor ink. No wonder corpses are editing my powers. (Begins to undo his trousers) So which sort of a priest are you - dehorned, bungling and kindhearted; a religious freak, towering and brittle; or the fun kind? (suddenly emphatic, looking at an armchair) *There* she is!

(Lord Cabell goes trouserless over to the chair, stands behind it and begins thrusting away.)

LORD SKYWAY (outraged): Is my view correct?

BARON ARBUSTO (disbelieving): Must I check every attitude?

LORD CARLYLE (flabbergasted): At last this criminal has decided to smash the world and his position in it!

CABELL (mildly): Harken, that wife of yours seems to be made of wax.

STRAUSS: Do you have nothing to say about your behaviour?

CABELL: Well, I'd rather not be doing it surrounded by spooked failures, but other than that ...

HARKEN: But in your defence, man! Tell us this is the first time!

CABELL: It is, as a matter of fact. And it's not that adultery business the padre mentioned, so his prediction was correct.

STRAUSS: 'Thou shall not worship false idols', then.

CABELL: It's true that I'm not worshipping this object, merely using it like a whore. Any objection to that? Oh I suppose I'm coveting this fellow's furniture am I? Lord Brickham - any objection to me plugging the old tadger into the backrest of this chair of yours?

BRICKHAM (vaguely): It's not an antique.

CABELL: There. I take nothing away, and if I retain enough control to withdraw at the prime instant, I'll leave nothing behind. Though my seed would doubtless add to the value of this stuffed wooden carcass for those in future times hoping to glean some clue to the habits of our shining society. History dries in your parlour, Lord Brickham.

ARBUSTO: Oh this bastard is intolerable. Get him out of here.

CABELL: What do you expect, Arbusto? A vacuum like this longs for profanity. Hup! Hup!

(They lunge at him and he dodges about, climbing over tables etc to escape them.)

STRAUSS: Your perversity has no label but it is perversity nonetheless!

CABELL: Why? Because my fidelity's more colourful than yours? (rambunctious) I sense a new sin in the making! What about this? (He springs up and grabs onto the chandalier, hanging by one arm and swinging like a monkey - his ears seem to be inflating like balloons and bursts of Tesla energy crackle and branch across the ceiling) Got a name for that? Or how about this? (As Cabell drops to the floor, from above a dozen Cabell lookalikes drop with him, scrambling immediately offstage) Or this one? (An upright coffin rises from the floor behind Cabell and he glides backward into it, the coffin slamming closed and sinking from view - Cabell enters stage right, smoking a cigar.)

SKYWAY: You bloody crook!

CABELL: Why so drunk, Lord Skyway? Consequences too scary again?

SKYWAY: How dare you, sir - who the hell are you?

CARLYLE: So what does it all mean, Cabell, this business?

HARKEN: Yes, Cabell - you've been building up our expectations like some sort of demented barber. What are you about?

CABELL: Something very particular. I intend to grow a limb which has no name in this world. One as alien as honesty, and as shocking. Look.

(As an echoey voice ululates from somewhere Cabell's chest swells, his shirt bursting open as a massive glowing green limb inflates several yards into the room, knocking over vases and furniture.)

CABELL: It's not competitive but it is playful.

(The others react with shouts and panic.)

CABELL: I could punch this hand between your shoulderblades and drag you through your heart backwards. (casually examining his cigar) But, I for one will breathe easier when ...

(He touches the cigar to the giant limb - it bursts with a flash of light, plunging the stage briefly into darkness. When the lights come back up, Cabell is gone but there's a frog on the table.)

HARKEN'S WIFE: Oh good grief, there's a frog on the table!

(Chaos erupts, everyone chasing the frog and declaring that the situation is intolerable.)

CONSCIENCE (Burroughsian universal voice): It's a fragile system in which a frog is an emergency.

FADE TO BLACK

GROUND WHALES

Seven burrowing whales were denied entry to a restricted bunker Thursday afternoon, during the worst snows to hit New Mexico in twenty-one years. Taos Sheriff Sam Edwards said he felt sympathetic to the ground whales, accepting that they may have been simply obstructed by the bunker, which exists for the protection of bureaucrats in the event of a nuclear strike. 'The burrower whales came up against the bunker wall at about 15.15, causing a general security alarm. A specialist mining contingent went below to guide the whales aside by taunting them and tying industrial tow cable around their beaks. The whales didn't say anything, because they never do.' When asked the precise form of the taunting, Sheriff Edwards refused to comment, except to say that the remarks were 'deliberately cruel to be kind'. He denied that he and others had taken shavings from the bonelike beaks of the rare ground whales, adding that if he had, he would now be 'obscenely rich'. Heavy snows hampered the work and twice the hydraulic winching rigs broke down, leading the Sheriff and his team to deliver a volley of abuse to TV crews and other bystanders - behaviour the Mayor has since dismissed as mere 'high spirits'. After six hours the subterranean giants were sent on their way, and Edwards has returned to the more mundane activity of sitting around in his car.

THE THINGS IN THE CITY
(after Lovecraft)

When I drew nigh the nameless city I knew it was accursed. I was traveling in a parched valley under the moon, and afar I saw the construct protruding uncannily above the sands as parts of a corpse may protrude from an ill-made grave. Fear spoke from the age-worn stones of this hoary survivor of time. I should have known that my brothers had good reason for shunning this sick place. The aspect of the spot was unwholesome, yet I longed to encounter some sign or device to prove that the city was indeed fashioned by reason. I sought some guiding principle, but all was chaos, retaining the crudity of the negligently left-off, the merely adequate. Its unsane edges stopped short without plan or sense, a jigsaw unrequited by the nature above and beyond it. Chambers and altars faced the world with the shabby incoherence of the mindless. I perceived with an unnameable horror that their foundations were as arbitrary as their spires. Only the most contorted artifice could manifest this unimaginable combination of sterility and necrotic corruption. It told of existence as a hammer, repeated doses of the same day, a desolation of such repetitive detail that I was almost mad with its ceaselessness.

Yet though the malignancy of the grey city was terrible - its airless aura sheened with a sweat like plastic, its roots without natural dust - far worse was the race that now emerged from the niches, all curiously low: a trickling pageant of monstrous pestilents. They seemed blindly automatic, hectic without joy. Fear had driven from me any vestiges of wonder, and now even this was supplanted by nausea, a soul dread of this acute, unconscious scourge. Worst thus far was the nightmarish impression of their spreading through weakness, withering unendingly outward. Swarming beetle-like with neither curiosity nor caution, wonder nor plan, eddying by the caprices of bureaucracy, sluggish yet unchecked, they moved by dilapidation, a decline they consciously denied. And then in a moment of indescribable emotion did I see within them a commotion which was also an emptiness. Those ant-like skulls yet held vaster abysses than those of remotest space; an uncomprehension less reverberate than unwalled infinity. They thrived without the redeeming colours and contours of fertility, for they perpetuated a void in which even the brightest of colours are bleak and the loudest of voices mute. Inarticulately spreading, a swarming negation to the cosmos, simultaneously feeble and raging, they left all they touched irrevocably tainted.

I fled that city as the far mountains drove the moon upward. And breathing into the huge darkness, I felt thankful to be what I was.

Since that freakish night I have studied the ancient records which tell of The Unfallen Empire, its tyranny of infinite repetition and its thin grey people. Whatever impulse compels them, there is no legend so old as to give it a name, or to recall that it was ever rational. Their menace is occulted because they hide it from themselves, twisting their motives so far aside of their sight that they are encircled with thorny evasion, a sickly black halo of barbs. Their very nature opposes the honesty of my kind, whose content is the same as our exterior and whose forms are as florid as our purposes. In their voracious toxicity, they are a lethality to all life. I dread them even as I lay dreaming.

HOROSCOPE

*Shock and appall your so-called friends by telling them
about the hell that awaits them.*

ARIES March 21 - April 21
You appear to be worried about your plan to steal from
the company, Aries. Do not be concerned. You will be
fired before the opportunity arises. Collect those crumbs
from your eye - they're trying to tell you something.
Despite bearing more than a passing resemblance to a
hen, you are despotic and surly. The world has already
lost patience with you and your so-called 'mystery ears'.
Skint in a tux, you impress nobody. Your diatribes send
passersby recoiling in disinterest. Yet believing the
patronising words of a professional, you will change
your name by deed poll to 'Babylon Tiger' and wear
some sort of wrestler's cape. In early Spring you will

slam into a bar full of mirrors, ferns, frogstands and icy women, vomit against the indoor water feature and wake up naked in a wild bird reserve. Your hoselike nose and tubular morality will not help you then.
Reading: Lady luck means to feed.

TAURUS April 21 - May 21
In February your head will twist open like a flower revealing a small platform upon which a puppetlike drama will unfold, toy maidens dancing about a well which is in fact the stump of your spinal canal. One of the tiny figurines will have the face of your father and as it quivers across the platform it will whisper 'Never to forgive.' And this is only one of the bounties awaiting you in the New Year, Taurus. Efforts of the past few years will finally pay off, as an eye defect will superimpose the image of flamingoes in surgical masks over everything you see. This will make your moods unpredictable and often dangerously explosive. You may learn that you can justify any atrocious act by connecting it with several years of a stranger's success - no-one condemns altruism.
Reading: Hang up the phone on a vampire - the definition of carefree.

GEMINI May 22 - June 21
Your crime will be discovered through carelessness. A single omission lays waste to many precautions. Not all publicity is good.
Reading: Fractured masks, the house empty.

CANCER June 22 - July 22
Put aside all doubts about your sexuality - the spaniel in question is The One. Yet an entrepreneurial enterprise which is close to your heart requires further consideration. There are no such things as 'Deluge Trousers'

and there never will be. Remember the tale of the man who, watching evenly-matched nuns in a bare-knuckle fight, bet on the one with the scariest face. Sharp bones are brittle! Consider every angle before making an announcement. You have shown taste and split-second timing before, Cancer, as when you pushed that waiter against the passing student.

Reading: Only the English clear heaven for dignitaries.

LEO July 23 - August 22

Couples: when feeding a guppy, spread the work - one to sprinkle the food, one to frown. You value domesticity, Leo, but sometimes you have to kick your heels and fire a gun randomly into a crowd. A brawl in a sawmill will leave you shaken and drenched with aviation fuel. Friends find your rage unfathomable and frightening - why not make amends? Avenge all wrongs against them, arriving unannounced and fluttering, orbiting the foe in jittery trouble, punching, punching. Take no credit for the vengeance. They will hear of their enemies' misfortunes and privately bless an angel. Love is granted before we know it, like an escaping bird. Respect is more slow, like a tired badger.

Reading: Tinsel on a man - happiness is dead.

VIRGO August 23 - Sep 23

You will develop the frictionless face of a dolphin and thus enter the bar at greater speed. All present will address you as a 'bottlenose bastard'. Incapable of human speech, you will not be able to order. The anecdote will flourish on the rubber chicken dinner circuit, bringing precious little benefit to you, Virgo. Yet in April your huge button eyes will fall upon a new love and romance will blossom. Understand that this is a time of regeneration. A man who believes in a billion things has a billion used tickets to sell. A clean slate

awaits the squeak of a lie - don't blow it, Virgo!
Reading: Whatever it purports to be, if everyone stops to watch, it is not advisable to drink it.

LIBRA Sep 24 - Oct 23

Arriving at work in early Feb, you will remove your coat and calmly push it into the mouth of your employer. Congratulations! Sympathising with their arrogance might encourage them to rule over you. Evade your responsibilities in March by mounting an adroit display of wasting sickness. A tip: cotton wool soaked in red dye looks like guts! Atone for your work by hurdling gravestones wearing a tail like an arrow. But beware - sooner or later the Court of Chancery will have you by the legs. The scales of justice mirror those of your own sign, Libra. Make a freak-show of your tears and tell them a fire-breathing wren told you to do it. This is the sort of nonsense of which courts are disposed to take a tolerant view. They'll send you away with pity and laughter. Unguarded remarks about Paul Scholes will earn you a smack in the mouth. Keep digging the tunnel.
Reading: Never refer to a large dog as a friend - he is in custody and he knows it.

SCORPIO Oct 24 - Nov 22

One of your henchmen will betray you to the fuzz. Saturn in Gemini in your second house leads to the confiscation of illegal earnings, which is how you could afford the second house in the first place. Traitors, all in rare form, are straining every nerve to keep from sniggering. In the festive season eleven bullets will unexpectedly take up lodging in your back. From your wounds the ballistic route will be triangulated to the fuzzy image of your mother, caught in the background of a tourist's snapshot. She is holding a rifle and has never looked so fulfilled. The corpse of your first victim will be dug up on a nutmeg plantation. A deposit of Iron Age snot will also be detected. In court your shouts of explanation will stray off the charted edges of the alphabet. 'Our only option was a grisly disposal at midnight' is no defence, Scorpio. Begging for leniency, you will come to regret that you have only two knees upon which to crawl. I see you in a turmoil of mistrust, weak amid a crowd of cheesy quavers. When you can't find your trousers but can find the front door, a message is being sent. Abandoned by all, you will spring off a building wearing a Hawaiian wreath of donor cards. Closed coffin if you get my drift.

Reading: Knives delight in a snug enclosure - for them it's freedom.

SAGITTARIUS Nov 23 - Dec 21

Saying 'Advantage mine' when overtaking someone on the pavement is not a winning attitude. Your pursuit of notoriety comes of the duty to compare. Your ideas end where most people's begin, Sagittarius. You kiss only the superior graves. You pretend to be a populist by fainting near a barricade. Serenity is painful for you. Status looks outward so unremittingly its heart may stop without concern. Pretty soon you'll be batting at invisible serpents. A faked photo of you with a smile and yacht bevy will be the last your friends hear of you. An obscure East End chef will serve an elaborate sugar sculpture of your arse. The first incision will reveal that the real arse rests within. Yet even this display of your charms will only reach the latter pages of the tabloids. Disintegration is the constant season.

Reading: Your contribution is condemned to the crowd.

CAPRICORN Dec 22 - Jan 20

In late November put it all on Deathbed Pioneer in the fifth at Haymarket - it's a lock. The optimist sees the future as a rabbit sees the oncoming truck - getting bigger, not closer. No sense getting all steamed up about things. Remember the philosopher Pandemal who went to hell with the words, 'Fatal place, have another bit.' Impish devilry is the order of the day, Capricorn. Attend the theatre in a waterlogged box jacket. Flick a poison spider into the orchestra pit. Slap a musician on the back so he gets his face caught in the thin end of the trumpet. Stare through a grating and frighten the children. Then sit and watch the money roll in.

Reading: Snack in a sniper's nest - calm before the storm.

AQUARIUS Jan 21 - Feb 19

You will celebrate Christmas Day under a fallen door. 'Freeze on day of purchase' - there's a grim double meaning there, Aquarius. Hesitation at the crucial instant releases mayhem, attacks by a screaming chimp, all poise lost. Feeble cries will bring eventual rescue and recovery in time for the multiple tragedies of the New Year.

Reading: A poet can often be found in a block of tar, still expressionless.

PISCES Feb 20 - March 20

The grim task of wedding a loved one is endured amid prolonged silences. This absurd and demeaning farce will take its toll on you, Pisces. A flower is coloured silk in the dirt, not a symbol. Cross the threshold of pity; can't get back across the armature. How to compensate for giving up a whole human in bits and pieces? Able to do anything, you merely answer the door. Talk of 'suction rhythm' will be met with a revolted silence. Escape, Pisces. Don't even make a scene. Punching a clown makes it hard to steer.

Reading: We bring death and those who claim to be our rivals bring death also. It's investing everywhere.

FULL BLOOM

A little gold cathedral spun down out of a sky blue as
an absinthe flame, settling its belly on the Whitehouse
lawn and sticking out its tongue. Photos of the woman
on the ramp were consecrated under headlines before
the chaos was locked down and the visitor transported
to a bunker under the streets of Washington. Some
observers could not conceal their disappointment at
her humanity, when they had innocently expected
a serrated lizard with fins galore. One expert sobbed
because she was nothing like a hammerhead shark.
The flying disc made it unlikely she was a random
nutter, but there didn't seem anything alien about her
except maybe those big eyes, and the travel armour she
shucked immediately: a purple-gold acid flake hinged
carapace with headlamps for breasts and a shoulder-
fender which flipped out to wings of semi-transparent

chrome. She stated impassively that she was from twenty-five years in the future. It seemed their belief was not required. When asked why her timeship was circled with Chinese symbols (rendered in green flake) and no Western writing, she stated that the building of the craft had required the backing of a world power.

She was tall, blonde, strong as metal cable, aged anything between thirty and fifty, and presented as American. She bore no explosive device or other weapon. Fearing that she was the weapon, they scanned her. She was normal, skullparts zipped together with calcium in the usual way. She carried no exotic disease. The factions argued, right and left money with right and left military. She observed calmly that this was a class distinction, and they stopped only briefly to hate her.

Her ability to casually exit locked rooms was embarrassing not because she could do so, but because to confront her on the fact would be to acknowledge they had locked the door. She always returned, and seemed to be waiting for something. Surveillance footage of her cell was marred by her sitting as still as a statue - observers watching her face for hours in close-up soon imagined they saw strange transformations in the swarming static. Sudden blank tape presumably concealed activity she didn't wish to broadcast. In any case their security was bankrupt, and attempts to shift or examine the time craft resulted in strange blackouts and loss of memory. The woman took one scientist aboard, who emerged describing something like a honeycomb of medals.

Attempts to gas her room or give her sedated meals resulted in her departure and days during which she was locked incommunicado within the disc. Her refusal to help them pretend they hadn't attacked her was the last straw for the military, and when she finally mentioned her name, intelligence came up trumps - she was a young girl living in Cleveland, unremarkable, with the seed of an interest in languages and no connection with the Orient.

Interrogation of the girl yielded nothing - she didn't know anything about her future self, and was merely frightened and worn down, especially when interrogation resulted in the loss of a kidney. But she and the older woman carried the same DNA.

Against scientists' objections that a meeting between the two was inadvisable, the girl was shown into a bare cell where the woman was sat at a metal table, the meeting observed and recorded through a one-way mirror.

She was surprised at the fragility of the young girl who uncertainly sat down across from her. Spiky, fibrous and yet to ripen, she was yellow in the head and filled to innocence with others' opinions. Etheric armatures of anxiety angled from her like insect legs. And strangely she had always carried within her the sweet and bitter secret that this, now, was the past.

She'd forgotten how terrible it was, the taste of youth in the mouth. The new-made jigsaw mask opposite made her relieved at her age. That she was wise enough to know she was being used, and that she could use it. With enough data to see at last the whole shape and put a cross through the centre of her life.

'I've learned a vast amount. Every life I've heard of has been a meaningless oblivion. But you and I together might accomplish something.'

She reached across the table for the girl's hand.

Something louder than sound was bending the window. Turning in mid-air, they were wrapped around eachother, arms and legs interwoven with the spiral of snow-white fire that coursed around and between them before exploding through the atomized glass. The blast blurred the bunker to dust and knocked an earthwave westward across the American continent. As the wave echoed back the land troughed open to a depth of four miles and, like a sandcastle moat, welcomed the filling sea.

PLANET

The planet was in fact a balled-up lobster the size of a planet. When it unfurled that tail, boy, to say we were surprised is an understatement. Freddy turned to me and raised his eyebrows, and had a slight smile on his face. It was a wild time for the boys. The very end of the tail looked like a red flattened fern. I remarked on it at the time because I'd flattened any number of ferns when I was a kid. Freddy challenged my interpretation and said it was like a set of russet feathers. Murphy ignored us, Fenchurch said we were both right, and Arlo was too busy screaming something about lobsters to contribute anything useful to the exchange. He was, in fact, always finding a way to avoid participation. Like the time he gasped something about a leak in the airlock seam and spent hours re-sealing the seam of the airlock while the rest of us were playing cards. We invited him several times to join us but he just looked blank, and even angry later on – as if he was above it. Now we had to try discussing this lobster situation above his bellowed technical suggestions concerning light-years and fanned laser bursts. 'We might tame it,' said Freddy, and started sniggering. No, I thought, we will not tame this. Its underside, previously hidden, was incredibly complicated with ribshapes and countless folded bony legs. I was sick and tired of it already. 'Let's just fly away,' I sighed, and that's how we decided. Arlo locked himself in his cabin, and when we knocked on his door at dinnertime, his muffled swearing assured us all he was good old Arlo, what a character.

THE BURNISHED ADVENTURES OF INJURY MOUSE

Bob became increasingly enraged at the other commentators and assured them vipers were utterly charming - he was married to one, in his mind. Basically, he said, yes basically, everything stemmed from that. There was utter silence after just a little of this. Bob thought it was hilarious, all of it. Why didn't these other guys try harder?

He was thrown out on his ass with no help from anyone - his conscience did it. *Oh my brothers*, he thought, smiling to himself, *that was your swansong, not mine.* And down the rain-oiled streets of that mooned evening he thought, *They'll have me back in a week, when they've forgotten.*

Snow fell in his memory, drifting him back to his imaginary childhood, and back again - which was warmer? That chill invention or these streets blistering with rain? Absolutely nothing constructive occurred to him. *There I am*, he thought - *a man of the times.* His coat was wool and coal and seashell. The sky was afterburn.

What a slick was here, pellucidant with rainlight reflection and coldness beyond his coat. Find a ghost in that, the rational would say, and out they'd come, unaware it had been rhetorical. Black trains steamed, stopped and oily, dinosaur trains, hopeless exhaust, explosions of rain over a missile body. Freight of dreams from wherever, nobody tried to unload anything - unscheduled stop. One man with an upholstered face squints out of a window closing up with ill-use and shouts he's 'Out of this world' or something similar, a very charming man anyway.

Failure is a state of mind, flummery and saline - drabness doesn't enter into the equation - look at those flowers - what flowers you say? Get the hell out of my way.

Ghosts from ghosts were born and from people were also born ghosts. All is diluted.

Bob underground thinks of these matters while making a replica of his brain from old clay. Some drops of moon water fall from the root-hung ceiling. They explode like mines on the broken floor, reminding him of the rain in shedsuburbs of blackberry tangle and compost rind behind wood.

All in a stale wet world of filigreed basement walls and runnelling alleys and lamplit mirth at the expense of failing actors and truncheon-wielding policemen who didn't then and don't now understand that life is a game for me to play and for them to lose.

Bob's book *The Day My Arse Exploded*, which detailed every way in which he was an 'extraordinary man', opened with a space-projected gamma-ray burst and its effects upon Bob's menagerie of slowly-wobbling latex badgers. Every chapter ended with the assertion that the events recounted therein explained why he was 'so surly'.

'I may be a failure,' he said, 'but I am a failure made of steel.' And he instructed the reader to march pugnaciously on the spot while chanting:

Chub learn from me
I learn from chub
But chub do not eat me
And that's the point.

'The gall of the man,' spat Curly, slamming the book and throwing it into the fire, which roared in a regrettably plastic grate. 'Reaching my silence, his blank predators devoured the time. Why did he release the bastards? Oh god - wife, the poison fumes from the melting grate!'

Betty entered with a statue of Lenin and stood there gazing. 'The smoke looks lovely doesn't it? Jade in colour isn't it?'

'I don't really know. Well, here we are again, uncertain!'

'Don't make such a scene Curly, we're polar bears.'

'I know that, but do they?'

'They will if you keep rolling around on the floor like that.'

'Look at me! Look at me!'

'Curly get up - get up!'

'I'm a bear everybody! A polar bear!'

'I can't believe this - after all those years being careful.'

The townsfolk squashed their faces against the windowglass like pressed flowers. Polar bears pretending to be people here in the simple house! Somehow liberty always resulted in this sort of thing.

'Raw deals are my vocation,' drawled the head of the

mob. 'Gimme an axe for the door.'

But the roof exploded and three bears, one a cub who waddled his legs as though running, hissed into the sky wearing vertical take-off jets. 'They're attached to the bears' backs with harnesses,' said the mob leader.

'That's the usual way,' murmured a town elder witheringly, and rueful sniggers rippled through the crowd.

It was decreed that a monument to the so-called 'flying bears' would be built upon the wrecked roof, and Jake the Fern was charged with the task of construction. He made jet contrails of wavey glass, surmounted with concrete bears. The entire construction was twenty-six feet in height, but the town authorities started asking him loudly what it was about, denying that they knew anything about the 'flying bears' and that they weren't paying for this piece of nonsense. Large crowds gathered to jeer at his crazy scheme.

But many crept back alone and confided to him furtively that yes, they remembered it all. Then they rushed away before they were seen with him.

What interested Jake was the fact that the bears were described by some of these witnesses as 'furry saints'.

It was not the first time Jake had been ill-used and burdened by the townspeople - the year before, he had been assured by one and all that the sum of seventy-three pounds awaited him in a fallen log near the Forest of Death. He was told he must carve the log into the shape of his 'fondest dream' before he could claim the cash.

But he became so obsessed with removing the money that he wound up carving a cash bundle to the exact scale of the one awaiting him within. The result was a set of rolled notes coated in a thin film of wood-fibre membrane. To remove the money would shatter his delicate work. When he looked up, he saw the townspeople crouching behind the bushes and sniggering in full knowledge of this common fate. A ceremonial old hag walked up and removed the wood-glazed wad from his hands, and Jake followed the slow procession down to a torch-lit underground chamber, where the object was placed within a rocky shelf with a hundred others. 'Here,' rasped the woman, 'bored with generosity, we consort with an institution of years. Make a bow to the many before you.'

'What?' asked Jake, too loud in the chamber.

The hag regarded him with distaste. 'Wearing a woollen jumper is like admitting you've killed for fun.'

And then all was celebration and distorted flame-shapes on the cavern walls. He awoke in a wet field halfway through the following day, and no-one ever acknowledged these expensive events.

So here he was with a set of concrete bears and no real excuse.

And on top of everything, he'd found a mummified hen in the mattress. Phoning his mother, he asked what a thing like that was likely to be worth these days. 'Unless it's covered in gold,' she said, pausing to drag on a cigarette, 'it's worth no more than you are.'

'You mean if I was covered in gold I'd be worth something?'

'I didn't say that.'

He phoned Bob. 'Bobby boy, I saw you on telly eleven months ago talking about vipers - the old noggin playing up again eh?'

'I meant every word - and it was last week, not eleven months ago.'

'Train me to understand.'

'Never ask that,' snapped Bob, slamming the phone.

Burning with inspiration, Jake pranced sideways, slamming against a small table. He had the idea that minnow-like things were running down a cable from the sun to his fragile head. 'Time is barren,' he gasped, 'we fill it with cheese triangles and nutty slack.'

'Baby,' he added.

Two days later he put his plan into action, wrecking everything he had achieved thus far. This act, anticipating the times, involved building a truck from sponge and scooting it against a load-bearing wall to the cry of 'Stay in the yard almighty.'

Everyone made such a fuss pulling him from the cab, pushing their fists against his nose and making sounds of anger, that he could not help but eject his brain. 'I'll pick it up later,' he assured them, swanning a short distance from the shocked crowd before going into a kind of fit. His arms windmilled and the torso region did nothing of interest as he voiced various concerns which were unfamiliar to the assembly. For instance, he mentioned his ability to 'kern' the face of a loved one so that she might more closely resemble a jaded merchant. He claimed there was a construction in the air which 'chaddered' the birds along if they were getting too sleepy or thoughtful, and swore he would smash it with his eyes. There were hordes of trendy majors hiding out in a nearby barn, he said, itching to make their appearance.

'Pelt me with pinecones,' he cried, but when the onlookers obliged he seemed taken completely unawares, focusing slowly their way as though surprised at their presence.

Jake spent a year travelling to see Bob. He travelled sitting in a shallow wooden crate with no wheels, its underside thickly coated with lard. On arrival he hailed Bob, entering the earthy cavern with the crate in his hands. 'Oho Bobby boy, I have travelled one year in this thing to see you. Give me something to eat.'

'Didn't you eat on the way here?'

'In the first week I ate the layer of lard from the crate's underside.'

'No lard then. Nor wheels. What were the means of propulsion?'

'My legs and my failure to understand certain principles.'

'Why did you sit in a shallow wooden crate and leg-shunt your way along for a year to see me.'

'I wanted to ask if you could record something for me off the telly.'

'Something a year ago.'

'I suppose so.'

'And you could have phoned me.'

'You're right.'

'Well, I don't have a video. Did you want anything else?'

'Not really.'

'Go then, and take your nostrils with you.'

'Those are my eyes.'

'I was pointing at your nostrils, now get out.'

Distant burst of screaming from the neighbours and I knew I was home, Jake wrote in his diary upon returning. *I will practice face-sagging for fourteen days and fourteen nights, in preparation for people's efforts to excite me. Then get back to work on the bears.*

But upon arriving at the bear house he found that the furry saints had been knocked away and replaced with noble effigies of the town council. Perched atop the glass jet-trail effect, these three were portrayed scratching localised dogma upon official tablets. 'What's this nonsense?' he asked, and entered the town hall naked for effect.

'Mr Fern is it?' asked the city father. 'Sit down, if you can. Some tea?'

'Get up, what are you waiting for, you want to hit me, go ahead like a man.' And Jake was shouting through the floppy movement of his own arms.

'It's from the heart, I can tell,' smiled the city man, 'but is it enough for me to sway forward from my comfortable chair, adjust my eyes to the new depth and so on?'

'You think so?' said Jake, confused. 'I'm accusing you of something. I knocked before entering.'

'And I thank you. That seems to conclude our business.'

'Bye then,' laughed Jake, and was standing on the wide stairs outside the building, smoking a black Japanese cigar.

The following day he returned with a dog, hammering at the locked council door until the dog became frightened and abandoned him. 'No use trying there,' smirked a squint of an old man who was sat on the steps. He stood and led Jake around the side of the building, pointing in through the window fog - inside, an interlocked forest of skeletons darkened the office. 'Good people,' nodded the man in approval. 'Certain of their position.'

But what's the good of thinking about it, Jake considered as he wandered home, and felt as if he'd learned something.

'What's this?' a copper demanded, pointing at a long swerving mark in the street.

'I did that pushing myself along in a wooden crate. It's been there a long time, old man.'

'Save your explanations,' sneered the copper, and was just winding himself up for action when a truck slammed him sideways out of view.

Jake was stopped by a man outside the bar. 'Buy this stone. It's carved from the biggest gem in the world.' And he showed Jake a crushed cigarette packet.

Considering his reply, Jake entered the bar and gave his order. He could tell the stranger that he was a married man, knotted and loath, with no time for finery. He could purse his lips, acting like a bird. Or he could stand utterly immobile, pointing at his own chops with his left hand. Plumping for the last, Jake finished his pint and went outside, only to surprise the stranger in the act of strangling a carp. Panicking, the man threw the carp into the sky, but it came down again, landing at his feet. 'I admit,' he said sadly, hanging his head, 'I serve Satan.'

And that's how it began. Two stupid men standing near a car without a clue what they were doing there. 'Abide back here, hopeless with us,' shouted the townspeople, and the pair wandered back inside.

'Like many dinosaurs,' Jake announced to the bar at large, lusty for a fine tale, 'the Tyrannosaurus appears incapable of discussing its feelings. Now there's one particular monster who -'

But before he could continue they turned their faces away, and Jake made a circuit of the room squashing those self-same faces against the walls so that they flattened to a pan. *If a thing's worth doing*, he thought, shouting with laughter.

Jake used a hand-cranked rendering mill to produce a fab new magazine called *Brain a Goat Snappy*. The first edition was in fact a shallow pizza box containing a herd of killer bees. The headline on the cover shouted INSIDE - KILLER BEES so when the creatures flew out and pelted the readers he could claim with the closed eyes of superiority that they had been fully warned. The second issue bore the headline INSIDE - KILLER BEES ON THE RAMPAGE and spoke mirthfully of the stress endured by the populace last time. The account was brought to life with vivid illustrations of O-mouthed fellows springing from armchairs in surprise at the approach of a bee - in order to make it clear that the object approaching was a bee, the illustrator had enlarged the insect to twelve times the size of the victim's head. Those scanning the account and its related diagrams were left in no doubt that an abomination had occurred, and Jake was arrested by a glass policeman full of sloshing liquid fat. All copies of the first edition were clumsily confiscated and Jake's lawyer asked what he planned to say in his defence. 'I will stand aglow,' Jake said, 'the wonder creeping abroad like a stench.'

'But you smashed the cop and released the liquid fat,' stated the lawyer, waving a tag of felt in Jake's face.

'Hello there,' said Jake.

In an effort to turn this verbal mistake to his advantage, Jake smiled at the lawyer in a way which suggested there was beauty in his arms, legs and motions.

'When you wrote that story about fluffy animals flying near people,' said the lawyer, 'did you think it was true?'

'I'm glad you noticed,' said Jake, and realising this made no sense, hastily added 'I love you' at a yell.

'I'm sorry Mr Fern,' sighed the lawyer, closing his briefcase and shaking his head. 'I now know what a monkey you are.' He walked to the door and turned back momentarily. 'Of course I'll bill you for the three hours we just spent chatting about energy fields.' And he left, leaving Jake in his legal office.

Jake became instantly excited, frolicking amid the files and throwing stuff at the ceiling. But while scrabbling across a desk as though swimming, he managed to push himself out the window.

'I plummetted eighty feet,' he told Bob later, 'and landed in the soft loving life of a beautiful woman, who said I was the best she'd ever had.'

'I happen to know,' Bob rumbled, 'that you landed in a pile of rubble and burning trash.'

'I'm alright though,' muttered Jake.

'I can sense that. Take a look at my knees.' And Bob sat on a wooden chair to be viewed.

'Your eyebrows, yes, so what?'

'My knees I said, as well you know. Look at them. Everything. Everything.'

'Steady on old boy.'

'Everything!' bellowed Bob, standing up, and advanced on Jake until the younger man was in the garden. The door closed and Jake was alone out there. Atmospheric changes of light, bird code ignored, and leaves to shade his eyes. And beyond the hedge, acres of solid fields. Who says mischief has no reward?

His next few issues of *Goat* contained the classic thoughtpiece 'Twenty reasons why I don't push carrots into my eye' (being actually the statement 'No time' repeated over and over) and the chicken series: 'Interpreting chicken', 'Why nothing can prepare you for chicken', 'You are tailormade for chicken' and the final in the series, simply, 'Horrorchicken'. His attempt to reach these heights again with 'Why I will never be a Majorette', 'Welcome to my treachery' and 'How to discern between me and your beautiful lover' were met with disappointment. Desperate to boost circulation, Jake set up a problem page, and the first question he received was: 'I have eaten a ton of lead. How many times have you done that?'

'Well, Seraphim,' he replied, 'many people see themselves as a dietary underclass because of this kind of practice, but not me. I can't get enough lead. In fact you'll likely find that your craving increases as the months and years pass. Crazy isn't it? My advice is to take a long hard look at yourself while spinning madly in a playground at night, while the rest of the world get on with their lives in a normal way. Looks like a crisis to me.'

Another reader stated: 'I was cooking a lemon when it suddenly exploded and took away half my face. What do you think of that?'

'It depends how you look at it - is your face half there or is your face half gone?'

He received a reply which re-stated that the man's face was half gone as a result of an explosion with a lemon. Abandoning the publication, Jake retreated to his diary: *Most people can't handle lead. Bake me ten pounds. I know everything that's worth knowing.*

And he ran out with a spraycan, writing MY ARM IS AT AN ANGLE on a high wall.

And he remained there for three days, trying to remember his name. Finally he went to a phonebox and called his mother, explaining he had to sign something. But ofcourse he couldn't tell her who he was, beyond 'Your fantastic boy.'

'What's fantastic about you?' she asked.

'I'm learning to fend for myself.'

'What else?'

'My legs are - wait, the money's running out!'

Calling back, he said 'My legs are long and tender, and I control them.'

But he'd dialled a local construction firm, and the reply he received was heartbreaking in its casual brutality.

He wrote in his journal that evening:

I lost a licence in a field
I picked a weed and gave it in
The notion of successful stuff
Left me

Terrapin rolled around and turned on the charm, but Jake was not in a social mood.

'I've got stigmata, baby,' he claimed.

'Where?'

'Right here.'

'That's your belly button.'

'I'll decide what it is. Did you hear me? I'll decide where and what it is. Now make some tea or something. This proves everything. Don't walk away.'

'You said you wanted some tea.'

'Alright you go and make your tea, that's right. But when I'm on the cover of *National Geographic* with this little beauty, don't crawl back saying you were with me all along.'

He looked at the newspaper. UNPLEASANT JELLY CLIMBS THE NATIONAL SUNLIGHT, went the headline.

And there was a sub-heading: IT SAPS MY SPIRIT ESPECIALLY, ROARS PM. Below the heading was a photograph of a wildly convulsing clown in an irrigation ditch.

'You cannot "lurch" masterfully,' Jake shouted through to the next room. 'That's what it says here. And acorns create dependable rooms. Small blazes jump and we feel dynamic. That's the spirit.' Jake gave it some thought. 'A pity that the truth is the exact opposite. Still, my neck is neutral.' He began sniggering.

Terrapin appeared in the doorway. 'So what do I get out of this relationship?'

'Shave a bee and find out,' Jake snorted, and cupped his face behind a chrome hand he had had smelted for the very purpose seven years previously.

'I need a thick metal hand to snigger behind when in the company of formidable women,' he had told a farmer.

'Why are you telling me?' asked the farmer, closing a gate on some cows.

'No-one else is interested,' Jake told him, and stamped his feet in the bitter cold. 'It's a bit nippy isn't it?'

The farmer pointed to a thin trough in the ground. 'The lobster march did that.'

'If you want me to believe you, I will.'

'It's true,' said the farmer, and opened a seam down the centre of his face - inside was a tangle of meat and veins, plus a brain the size of a marble. No wonder people walked the country to forget their worries.

The farmer was taking the situation very seriously. 'What a pity you won't feel responsibility for your actions. We'll have two long conversations, and one big fight during which I'll die of a fractured skull. Blame will fall on me. So you'll forgive me if I say goodbye now and avoid you forever. Goodbye.' And the farmer began to stride blindly away, falling almost instantly into a trough.

Parking outside the slaughterhouse, Jake erupted with laughter at thinking about the demonly-spiteful joke he would play on his friends and colleagues when he decided what that joke would be, and how everyone would scream at his wilfulness and then subside into laughter and relief when they realised all was in fun, all was not final or deadly and he only meant to break a few bones which could be re-set under favourable conditions. But he accidentally walked past the entrance and entered an alley full of dogs, which looked up in surprise.

Bruised afternoon, blood stars the basin - next time just nod, Jake wrote in his diary that evening.

So here he was in a serious relationship and nothing better than a metal hand for protection. The wonders of his newspaper were brutally rejected. *Well,* he thought, *they didn't like the truth, I'll give them truth. A small brown banjo is flourished at my head and I'm on the rug, at local expense. Let's see what they make of The Burnished Adventures of Injury Mouse.*

Feeling at the peak of his powers, Jake wrote the following:

'Painting the heads which rolled from the guillotine, Ted chose the colour blue. Because, he told the mayor, it's the colour of justice. The mayor believed him ofcourse, but really it was because blue was the colour of Elizabeth's eyes. Later, queries bowled down the bar like liquor. "I'll have a sliced eye," I say to the barking sarge behind the bar, "and a pair of calipers to hold it with." The barker looks at me as though from the belly of a wicker man. "Energy?" he ullulates mournfully. "I've no energy." Nelson would turn in his grave.'

'Where's the mouse?' asked Bob, scrutinising the manuscript.

'That's right,' Jake nodded, and snapped the piece from Bob's hand. 'Oh you consider a missing mouse condemns a tale of this quality.'

'You did call it *The Burnished Adventures of Injury Mouse*. Don't you care about anything?'

'I care,' Jake rumbled. 'And that's just the start. I'll change everything you've grown accustomed to. Fins on houses. Twitching elders. Slimline monkeys for narrow abutments. Because inside every packet o' bird verte-brae there's a ... *chhhhrrrrist!*'

The rage in this whoop scared Bob to the cells - could it be Jake was truly mental at last? No - he had found something in the packet. 'Free gift?'

'It's rather more complicated than that,' Jake whis-pered, and held up a tiny x-ray of his own legs. It was the size of a trading card. 'And there's writing.'

'What does it say.'

Jake held the scan up to the light, squinting. 'It says, "With Nat Adderley on cornet."'

Bob remained expressionless. 'Are we about through here?'

DOWNLOAD SYNDROME

(also known as: Upload Syndrome, Notehead, Power-point Paralysis, Appiness, It's In My Machine, Text Me, I'm On a Train, You've Lost Me, What, Void, Delegation)

Country of Origin: United States

First Known Case: Arthur H. McCollum, a meticulous note-taker and archivist who in 1939 was sectioned after flipping out alone in a funhouse. It transpired that he felt the need to instantly record or verbally relate everything that occurred to him physically or mentally. Dropping his notebook when surprised by a ghoul and thus unable to record or pass on his experiences, McCollum had subsequently undergone mental over-load through the remainder of the ride, emerging with foam spurting from his gob like a bath toy. Dr. Wilhelm

Reich concluded that McCollum had been involved in 'preventative archiving', the passing off of thoughts and experiences the moment they have occurred. McCollum thereby sought to maintain an almost totally empty mind. 'He regards the long-term harboring of thoughts,' wrote Reich, 'as a nuisance at best and at worst a violation.' The bulk of Reich's papers on the condition were lost in the Food & Drug Administration's burning of his literature in 1959. Since then advances in technology have facilitated an epidemic of the syndrome.

Symptoms: 1. Constant talking with aid of cell phones and email; 2. near-zero memory retention; 3. dead stare; 4. blithely confident attitude.

Development, Cures, and Comments: The habit of thinking and recalling in their appliances rather than their own heads has left the greater proportion of the populace as empty, predictable and available as an arcade duck. Even when mismanaged into a moment alone the sufferer will state where he is and what, if anything, he is thinking. For millions the reluctance to introspect has led to the actual inability to do so. For others the world has always been so. The archaic practice of contemplation is not missed by those who, having never had an original idea, have never gotten a taste for them. They will speak of celebrity or, when pressed, mini-veggie preparation. Conversation is a brush of tumbleweeds, lacking all anecdotal detail, as in: 'This guy was, like, "Hello?" and I was like, "Excuse me?"' It becomes entirely reasonable to say in surprised exasperation, 'How do you expect me to remember something we talked about *half an hour* ago?' As Ken Stinnett bellowed from the upper ledge of a burning cathedral last year, 'Since the procedure which has become known as "giving it the wave-through" or simply "voiding" has become common behaviour, churches and multinationals have never looked back. The masses trample themselves in their rush to forget. Yes, my beauties, dispute my fury and I'll really commence. A man lives dilute, his death is a watercolour, we look upon it and pretend to learn. Pieces of law as medals, that's as fertile as it gets. Tomorrow-dollars met our eyes for years before we realized they weren't getting any closer didn't they? So I'm naked, so what? Oh, here come the cops, what a surprise. Peering at my expertise eh madam? I don't blame you. These are dry times and getting drier. The wrong solution closes the curtains, a slumber less natural than death. Eh, what? Cease and desist? What kind of yammer is that?' Stinnett's words were confirmed by his subsequent slaying by police and the blank stare that greets the mention of his name today. Research into nerve interfacing continues apace. Technologically, the ideal is to record all thoughts before they can surface to inflict texture and mayhem on the conscious mind. The pursuit of a cure is becoming hourly less a matter for urgency. A cure for what? Something forgotten. We are faced with the 'I am Legend' paradigm. When the majority of the world population suffers the same condition, does it become the 'new normal'?

STINGRAY VALENTINE
(intro to DH Wilson's Scikungfi Trilogy)

Certain memories become sacred. In DH Wilson's case it was the time he tripped and fell into an ancient liturgical drama, swearing point-blank into the face of a bishop long dead. He then wounded nineteen people while running amok in that antique realm, as the metal-clawed creature later known to history as 'Spring-Heeled Jack'. Thus he knew paradise and lost it. Wilson is now as helpless before the dictates of his moods and whims as he was before the violent wormhole calamities of childhood. But that is unimportant. What matters is that he exists and that he was made aware of the fact before we were. Everyone has experienced the dismal waste of time that can be inflicted by those who wish us to know them before they know themselves. This is a crime for which Kermit the Frog has yet to be punished, unless you count the fact that he can't stop moving his arms.

It is not unusual for the memory to condense into a single mythical moment the contingencies and practicalities of artistic inspiration. Wilson claims he decided to write his barbaric and erudite Scikungfi Trilogy while trying to inflate some sort of pool toy, an exercise at which he repeatedly failed until collapsing into tears, a pathetic sight for one and all. That crude vinyl icon of a camel, dented and lopsided, hung from his lap like every failure in his life. Wilson's life can indeed be divided into two parts: before and after this sacramental defeat. It was a bankruptcy localized enough to be effective – effortlessly checkmated by a novelty plaything, what could he do but overcompensate, creating a mental yakuza in which he could demand massive respect? The accident rivetted him to a public downfall like a voodoo chicken to the door of a Catholic priest, who gratefully cooks the mascot for his happy family. The scornful gaze of Wilson's friends as he let the flaccid toy slip from his slack hands transformed him into a constituted nature. He dreamed of a world in which his powers – those of the mind – are respected. Such a world does not as yet exist, but he can imagine one in the very mind that desires respect – thus creating a vortical involution resembling his inefficiently pursed lips during that initial washout of an afternoon.

We can surmise that this decision will be of capital importance – to say, in defiance of all, I Will Not Merely Be a Beaky Buffoon For You Bastards. Rather than a journey to the end of his misfortune, he invents a way out via a character who can make a blow to the face last a week. An altar of asphalt and sugar bulges from Wilson's fireplace, embedded with femurs and vintage Vickers ammunition belts. He can immerse his books in concrete detail – coincidentally a fate the mob have had in mind for him since he crashed one of their meetings in a monster truck and leaned out to explain that the universe is 'not motivated by obligation – where's your Omerta now?' Such mad confidence within despair will bear grim fruit. It spies on its own inner life and discovers electric mischief elves pounding up eternal-repetition exit ramps aglow. To the right-thinking man these denote only psychosis, yet these are what Wilson offers to others in the guise of 'supporting players'. Sure of possessing the ground spice created from exploding truth at supercompressed angles (actually the corner of someone else's barn) and concerned only with being seen in this undertaking, he expects to be tolerated. If he looks at himself in this mirror, he sees the accelerated colours of his magically-clad transparencies, at vertices to each other and tagged with self-triggering name-clues that should be obvious to you, reader. We have seen that as a result of his multidimensional misfortunes as a child and his public inadequacy as an adult he has dreamed of raising himself above men. Despite the daily battering of a thousand bitter truths, this dream has never left him. Society, too, defends itself against the barrage of facts present and latent in the universe, against the numinous and the precise, by means of custom - that is, by a body of consensual observances. Inversely, infraction of the customary rules invests the offender with a sacred aura because it confers upon him the power to unloose truthful powers – though whether he chooses to use his oblique position for this purpose is another matter. In *Tarka the Otter* we find that Henry Williamson has used the outcast position merely to talk about an otter and 'his joyful water life', deftly skirting the explosive issues of scorching sedition and profanely exotic rebellion almost any other writer would have explored.

Not all prose springs from the intention to communi-

cate - whether it be meaning, disease, magnified trucu-
lence, secrets manufactured specifically to be revealed,
a market mysticism of betrayal, centuries interrupted doom plots at last resumed, the innocent back of a
monster, sham delights, appliable death-blows or the
custom joinery of Trojan-viral prayer. Those who have
drugged furniture, diabolified dialogue and sacrificed
storyline in a desperate attempt to stray from current
literature's cheap, worn paradox and pre-explained
heroes deliver a merciless cure, a dimly-lit liberation
that leaves the reader with the final responsibility to
walk away from this trash-catharsis and start using his
or her brain, if only in miniature. Beyond this the fren-
zied and exacting works of quantum pointillists such as
Jeff Lint, Violaine and Eddie Gamete leave their stains
at the high-tide mark of psychodimensional exploration
where no one thinks to look.

Wilson's propulsion from hydraulic misfortune to a
rambunctious form of expression, his spirited attempts
to wear the reader's face for a hat and the final, very
public siege and arrest which exposed both him and
his doll-filled basement to the American media, are now
well-known. There is a thriving market – from which
he does not profit – in t-shirts bearing the notorious
mug-shot in which he is seen to have twelve eyes,
all of them closed. The trial itself is better known for
the sudden exhibition of Wilson's 'energy snake' than
any meaningful discourse on literature. My hopes for
an awakened interest in hypervortexal fiction came to
an end with that childish display and the subsequent
descent into flailing drop-kicks and hollering ushers.
Since the debacle Wilson has been publicly defined as
a snorting disaster-pig and his technical and creative
gifts have been relegated to the realm of myth (or what
Marshall Hurk has called 'the secret place of honour').
It is hard to gauge how it has affected his personality,

just as it is difficult to measure to the millimeter the distance travelled by a swarm. Certainly he could never sustain the half-mad state of nervous excitement he displayed in the courtroom. In recent photographs he stares as if stunned by a blowfish.

Although Wilson will no doubt remain an enigma to some, as one who has made a tremendous contribution to the immense story of human violence his work is sure to generate frantic evasion and nervous disdain amid the follower-filled timidity of modern scholarship, and a wide readership among the groundlessly triumphant, the conspicuously fanged and the seeking.

The public image of The Author - ramrod straight, unsurprised and studded with snails that make a popping sound when removed – has given way to the general impression of a force intent on using as many words as possible to say nothing we don't already know. It's a choice between those who were once alive or those who are now dead. Faced with an industry impermeable to talent, real creators will turn in another direction and aim at a heightened target, a unique emblem all bedecked with resinous blossoms and chained fruit. It may feel like a mixture of a stingray, a valentine and a nasty bump on the noggin. An abyss of treasure, detail-rich and explorable at every scale. For myself, I would ask a favour of everyone reading this introduction. If you're going to write, write something interesting and original, or get the fuck out of the way.

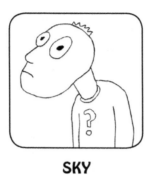

SKY

It was the most boring flying saucer I'd ever seen. And it wasn't even a flying saucer, it was an aeroplane. But I saw it, and that's me. Every time I look up, there's something. Clouds, some sky, the edge of a tree. Sometimes a bird. Why all the alternation? I was pretty sure it wasn't being done for my benefit. And something taking that much effort and organisation couldn't be a chance affair. I decided to record what I saw in a notebook I called MY SKY PROBLEMS and lucky I did. Pretty soon a pattern developed - for a start if I counted white sky and blue sky as two different objects. A dash dot morse code jamboree was playing out over my head and I wanted to know why. After three years of this business I was all full of beans about my results and tried to tell everyone, who mostly punched me or at least looked away. I spent a long time decoding it and after getting rid of a lot of nonsense it came down to one thing, a message from maybe god or the nature above us loud and clear: 'Look out below for everything you mothers because I hate you all and am determined to first fry you and then freeze you and soak you all in a short period of days and I remind you you're not just meant to get used to it. I been planning this for years and now I will unleash upon you everything I just said. Pay me attention down there. Hey down there, hey.' But even science article magazines did not care for my decoding of what I see every day. Clouds, some sky, the edge of a tree. Sometimes a bird.

SPECTER'S WAY

When Sam's apartment was burgled, he called the police. You might ask why he tried such a daredevil stunt. He knew some martial arts but was so slow that in any given fight he reacted to the blows thrown in the previous one. Faced with seven cops, he was punched in the nozzle several times and didn't recover especially fast.

He wasted a phone call on his girlfriend. 'Pam, I got robbed.'

'You're in *jail*? I am *super* fucking angry at you Sam.'

So it was at least a day later that an autolawyer was provided. Harpoon Specter popped into the office of Police Chief Henry Blince and sat smiling on the corner of his desk. 'I hear you got my client on a Peter Watts, Chief.'

'A charge of assault is standard procedure after we assault a civvy, Specter.' Blince's smile made his cigar rear. 'Your client's charged with burglary, assault and going with intent to commit sundry offences. If these symptoms persist - and it costs practically nothing to cure them - he'll bleed out unattended.'

'Yes. What a disaster it all is.'

They had a good laugh about that and were still laughing when a gang of troopers dragged Gecko Jeff past the door and Blince hauled his bulk to investigate. The troopers had Jeff against the wall and were mashing his face this way and that so he more resembled the photofit from the burglary. The rat-like Jeff reached up and pushed his nose downward. 'B-but if you squash my nose like this -'

'Quiet!' Blince shouted, lumbering over. 'Pull the cheeks out more, Benny boy! Not like that! Ah, this is gonna be tough.' He shook his head. 'Well, I guess we'll get it in editing. Put him in the cell.'

'You'd pay to synchronise him permanently, Chief?' asked Specter, who had been looking on.

'Remember old Klepp's Law, that mass human cruelty doubles every eighteen months? Plastic surgery's quick and inexpensive these days, Specter.'

Blince returned to his desk and sat heavily. Anyone on at least nodding acquaintance with gravity would have given him a year to live, but he had more than a decade ahead of him. An artist called Bud Dajo had once made a time-lapse video sequence of cops solving crimes - a strangely flickering officer sat at a desk for what seemed like only a year or two. But the movies included so many subliminal flashes of cops committing crimes of their own the video was banned. Dajo himself died in a voting accident and no one had noticed anything special about him since.

'Your man's alibi, it's like a mast on a coffin. If this

guy's a crazed killer - and there is no reason to believe he's not - he's out there running on revenge fumes, comes chargin' out of the gate and beats up a buncha cops, that's the killin' jar right there.'

Specter smiled. 'He may not see it that way, Henry.'

'He broke my arm and jabbed my eye. I can't stand for such things, as a rule.'

'You look fine.'

'That's a pretty flip attitude.'

'Maybe you could stand the exercise. Anyway, I value your comments, Henry, and I don't want to antagonise you, but I need to know are we gonna prosecute under political laws while not accepting a political defence or under criminal law while accepting a political prosecution?'

Blince scrutinised his cigar. 'There are no other options.'

Sam's face had long since given up caring what direction it was pointed in. Sat at a table in the yelling cell, he barely acknowledged Gecko Jeff when he was forced into the chair opposite. But similarly snagged in the law's perplexity ordeal, they had at least that in common. Gecko Jeff showed how he could bulge his eyes in a startling way, and by doing so out of context during conversation, stop everything. Sam talked about how he met his girlfriend. 'Circumstances conspired to have me acting normal, entirely by accident. And that's when she saw me.'

Pretty soon they were laughing about the sign on the wall that said IF YOU CAN READ THIS, YOU'RE IN JAIL. But Sam became thoughtful, telling Jeff to simmer down. 'Jeff, listen to me. What are the chances of two people this stupid meeting up?'

'In a world like this...'

'Don't understand me too quickly - think about it. We could have spent our whole lives eating pasta, jogging, and probably - almost certainly - never have been lucky enough to meet one other being like ourselves. Yet here we are.'

Jeff looked blank. Sam grinned.

'I tell you the combined stupidity in this room is ... probably unprecedented. I follow a cult, don't you?'

'Yes,' Jeff gasped.

'There you are. And I'll bet you play paddle ball, vote Republican automatically, and think Staind are alternative.'

'Ofcourse.'

'You see? Neither of us have ever had a thought of our own.'

'You're thinking this.'

'This is trash,' said Sam cheerfully.

'I guess so.'

'We could eat our own legs. Me and you. Right here.'

'Yes. We *could* eat our own legs.'

'But first dosing them with poison,' Sam laughed.

Jeff giggled with him. 'And branding them with Nazi insignia!'

'The coroner would be baffled!'

'So would we!'

Specter entered with a bundle of papers. 'Now now, what are you morons laughing about? Planning to eat your own legs?'

The clients' mirth halted abruptly.

'Seen it all before.' He seated himself at an adjacent chair and flopped open the case folder. 'But it does you a certain amount of credit to keep your legs hidden under the table this way. Hell, I'll bet there's alot about your legs I don't know. Me, I'm amazed by my arms. I sometimes have myself woken in the night just to look at them.' He frowned at the files and spoke absently. 'But legs? I'll bet you saw straight away I was the sort of guy who when I left the room you wouldn't remember how many legs I even had.' Satisfied at his reading, he became brisk and looked up at them. 'Now. My plans for your case are so big they'll have to be formally submitted to the city and everyone will be issued with safety goggles. I've already shouted something about the incomplete design of their myths, the first thing that came into my head. I threw a sort of flamboyant tantrum in the corridor, insulted the Chief of Police in several styles hoping to score a hit - and while that was happening I looked around and couldn't find anyone who disagreed with my opinion. Then I said some things I'm not proud of.'

'Like what.'

'I told Chief Blince that he was using a brain that was several times too small for him, and that humanity created a larger belly for itself because of some misunderstanding about the invention of the wheel.'

'That doesn't sound too bad.'

'Then I set fire to his chin, or tried to. Anyway, I have been instructed by my mind to adopt a particular strategy for you. It's what I call Sudden Death Advocacy.'

'What does that entail?' Sam asked.

Specter sighed. 'Exactly like it sounds, Mr Cutshaw - as I give forth in the perjury room, you suffer a sudden death - or appear to. I'm going to dose you with a powerful sedative which mimics the symptoms of mortification. For you it'll be like a night at the opera without the squirming. For me it'll mean an end to a hopeless case, and we ship you over the border in a crate of apples. That's how it's been done for years. Law and justice - keep them at a distance and they look alike.'

'What happens to me?' asked Gecko Jeff.

'You both appear to die. I've taken on both cases - there's no conflict because according to the records you, Jeff, were doing a different burglary that night over at the Jonsi place.'

In fact since the Completion, at which everything had been deemed illegal at last, the law was so entirely stacked in the authorities' favour that any lawyer arguing lawfully could be said to have a conflict. But in this regard Specter would describe a necessary loophole at the end of this very case.

'Let me get this straight,' said Sam, and repeated Specter's narcolepsy plan precisely word for word, though with a different expression on his face and with certain yelps and screams of intonation that made it clear the plan found no favour in his mind. Jeff concurred, uncertainly mimicking some of the yelps.

'You don't know what's good for you,' Specter urged. 'The brotherhood are big-picture guys - they're not much into detail.'

'We just want to be free.'

'As do we all. Yet what strange paths you are taking toward that goal. Well, it's a bonehead play but you're the clients.'

They started with motive or, in Chief Blince's words, 'Why he would want to do a thing like that.'

'According to the Chief's note in your file, "We tortured him but he refused to comment." This alibi of yours is hideously run down, Sam. Jeff's, on the other hand, is comedy gold. Maybe you could swap, and he'll take a percentage of the margin. Which course of exhaustion do you favour?'

'I'm a chef. I only sporadically renew contact with reality.'

'I defended a waiter once. He told me "My job is to take your order, put it together and then give it to you in a container from which it cannot escape." Trapdoor to his feet, he was still refusing to repent. I'm of a positive mind, Sam. Rather than being baffled at your behaviour, I prefer to think of your motivations as rich in mystery.

Let's say you were somewhat indignant upon finding that the crime had already commenced prior to your arrival.'

'That certainly shows a lack of regard.'

'He catches on fast, this one. We're making progress. Jeff, let's take a playful romp through this alibi of yours. The getaway. I see you changed cars during the chase - into exactly the same kind of car and even the same colour. What was the point of that? And looking at the item list here, a rabbit with ears like chainsaw covers - why did you steal the bunny rabbit?'

'The sun was in my eyes - check the layout of the Jonsi house, there's a window right over the bureau.'

'If I can establish the sun's angle at that time ...' Specter trailed off into silence.

'What?'

'Facts. We don't even mention them if we can help it. They don't match the ambience during trial - you'll see what I mean. The judge is basically a modified wardrobe and a domed forehead stuffed with god knows what. Not to mention a nose that wouldn't disgrace a demon of the underworld.' Specter stopped for a reaction. He was never really prepared for how uninterested people were to hear this.

'But I was never at Sam's house,' said Jeff.

'Facts, facts! Maybe you self-sabotaged? Maybe your needs are evolving? Being a resilient man, you broke into someone else's premises for prayer and reflection. Which I know you can do. And that was your first mistake. The greater distance between combatants, the more legal it is. Look at surgical strike missiles. Unfortunately you and the cops were right amongst eachother. You're in the soup, both of you.' He gave them a look of doom, then snapped out of it. 'But we mustn't think that way. Let's get some coffee on and go back over this a little. We got a lot of things that don't add up, but let's have a go.'

Four hours later Sam and Jeff were in a trance of despair. Specter stood cheerfully and packed away the files. 'Now I need you to think about visual presentation in court. Long earrings frame the face. And Sam, it imposes no strain on my credulity to believe that your head is made of cork. But if that's the biggest thing you've got to worry about, you're alright. If they point a gun or some sort of spear at you, change the subject. This forlorn and undermined thing you're doing won't play, however. Trial's tomorrow. I was loyally dismayed, I assure you. There's a vogue for dismay right now so it went down well. There's more to representing a client than winning a case.'

'Like what?'

'See you tomorrow.'

'In the empty space where a nightmare is stalling, when a dream fails to conceive, this court is back in session.'

'Guess how I've been distorted today,' Specter whispered aside to his clients, but was suddenly called to sum up.

He stood, unbuttoned his jacket, strode a little, buttoned it again.

'I look about me,' he began, 'and what do I see. Wood panelling: the decor of resignation. These two doomed men I represent. A jury, for all the world like goblins who have toddled out of chubby houses. You, your honour, as creepy as a dead man's glasses. And your wife - a creature you apparently met while ice fishing. I have no objection whatever to this little comedy. But the lives of two men are at stake. We have heard that on the night in question they accomplished theft, assault, grand larceny and murder. Let us think about that afternoon, those of us who are capable. Flushed cauls hung on like jellyfish and cells went off in coffins. Ecclesiastical profiteers adjourned to pray to the creature styling itself god at the time. And Gecko Jeff, this living ingot of pugnacity over here, vaulted the balcony of the Jonsi house, for a burglary he carried out at his own expense. In case it didn't work out, he hadn't told anyone what he was doing. You may retort, this guy had a top-notch idea for a burglary and no right to keep it to himself. And so he didn't. Witnesses said the thief "oozed self-confidence". And so he did. He was as happy as a dog on a Ferris wheel. Shortly thereafter, Sam Cutshaw - this man - instigated a brawl with the police by calling them on the phone and having nothing to pay them upon arrival, because he had been robbed. Ears are silent - the ultimate irony. Yes, they were arrogant. Yes, the robbery took a nasty left turn. And Gecko Jeff denied it all - yet his account was not a lie but a "re-imagining" of the event. I don't want to be drawn into an argument about the guilt or innocence of these boys or a determination of the facts. Let us not suffer unnecessary complications. The time for an objective account of these crimes, and who should be punished for them, is still far in the future. But look at them as they sit here. Lives built on a bedrock of setbacks and exasperation, they measure distance in barstools. Offer them a chicken wing and they'd bite it out of your hand so fast it'd blow the hat off a picture of Our Lord. Sneaky, ashen and without insight, refuge from causes of anguish, redeemed by nothing, they sit awaiting - what? Even the most casual survey of their faces reveals the strain and sadness of the innocent. Yet the police claim that they and their murderous ways have caused delay after expensive delay. No, nothing about this adds up atall. And since the Completion we're beyond measuring fine tolerances. I've consulted the book of transient reproaches -'

'He means the law,' explained the judge wearily.

'You seem determined to have no curiosity on the matter, your honour. Watch out! You know why? This microfossil of a principle you live by - perhaps it's better than nothing, perhaps not. But even you will be erased, along with your sky-high game scores. It's a pretty tough dollar in this town. In fact you have to print them yourselves eh, ladies and gentlemen of the jury? We expect ourselves, like our illusions of justice, to be arrested now and again for a very short while - only to return to our cotton-wool fantasies of hope. Laws - the common folk have been able to further their growth, but have no real part in them. Before the Completion, some of the fresher laws were recourses minted in panic or floundering embarrassment. They at least had a human feel. Now, with everything illegal, the city's flat, like soda with the lid left off. A world clinically de-aquefied of meaning. Philosophers whose names would mean nothing to you have asserted through the ages that god has fashioned a world detailed enough for everyone to find something to object to. Perhaps the time truly will come when the universe is packed solid with flags.'

Saying this, he appeared to modify the air in front of him with an arcane motion of his hands.

'And now you'll want to know my conclusions. I thought up the wildest schemes and the most crystalline for pulling the wool over your eyes. I decided, in proportion to my understanding of events, to reframe the confrontation as a kind of offputting dance or shabby flirtation. I'm as surprised as you are. Human beings are eccentric among the apes but commonplace among demons. If we blow the dust and snot from antiquity's archives we see that the ancients had already reached this conclusion and moved on to less obvious affairs. We shop; we laminate nature for ease of enjoyment. These men acted while the balance of their minds was disturbed - that is, during that long moment between birth and death. There is every reason to suppose that my assertions won't be believed. But this here is different from the relationships that we finish without solving. No butterfingered departure this time. Capital punishment - execution - is the kindest thing, as who would want to live in a world where people, even the innocent, are executed? So there it is: a defence as entertaining as it is informative. And I hate you all.'

Specter sat down. He leaned aside to whisper to his clients. 'Time to throw a rope over a pipe.'

Jeff sat insensible.

'That's it?' asked Sam, dazed. 'But...'

And he had to force his way through the palpable postmodern fog that existed in every court room. His mouth rebelled but he stated it clearly. It physically hurt.

'But ... I'm the *victim*. And they beat the hell out of me.'

Specter seemed not to hear. But he spoke, without looking at him. 'There is another law.'

'Another one?'

'The oldest.'

'Will it help us?'

'Thermodynamics. Whereby those who enforce the law cannot possibly be acting against it.'

Specter stood and addressed the room. 'Nothing further.'

'The Retrial' first appeared in *Interzone*, 2005.

'Download Syndrome' first appeared in *The Thackery T. Lambshead Pocket Guide to Eccentric & Discredited Diseases*, 2003.

'Bossanova' first appeared on *Quercus SF* online, 2004.

'The Man Whose Head Expanded' first appeared in *Perverted by Language: Fiction Inspired by The Fall*, 2007.

'On Reading New Books' first appeared in the *Tao Te Jinx*, 2004.

'The Things in the City' (after Lovecraft) first appeared in Saucytooth Webthology online, 2009.

'The Burnished Adventures of Injury Mouse' first published in *Bust Down the Doors and Eat All the Chickens*, 2009.

'Stingray Valentine' first appeared as the intro to DH Wilson's *Codename Prague*, 2010.

'Evernemesi' first appeared on *Beat the Dust* (online) 2009.

'Voyage of the Iguana' first appeared properly in *Fast Ships, Black Sails*, 2008.

'Whisper' first appeared in *The Flash*, 2007.

'Horoscope' first appeared in the *Tao Te Jinx*, 2004.

'Specter's Way' first appeared in *Crimetime* (online) 2010.